PRAISE FOR *EQUIPPED*

Spiritual warfare is a constant in the life of all followers of Jesus. This book is built around acknowledging the reality of that warfare and reminding Christians of the tools given to them for the fight. Continually bringing readers back to their identity in Jesus and the armor given to them, this book will benefit those whose eyes are just opening to spiritual warfare for the first time and those who are weary from the fight in which they have been engaged. An incredible resource for the Church.

—Ted Doering, pastor of Narrative Lutheran Church
and co-author of *Myth of the Millennial*

If you ever believed that Christians simply had to absorb the devil's attacks, *Equipped* gives us permission to fight back! Through this frontline soldier's resource on spiritual warfare, Pastor Kennedy offers novel insights into each piece of God's armor. His thought-provoking questions challenge us to identify spiritual attacks, which piece of armor to deploy, and how to engage in the good fight of faith, trusting Christ to lead the charge. One by one, he methodically strips away the devil's deceitful masks and replaces them with the blood-bought truth about our holy wardrobe. Pastor Kennedy delineates modern-day scenarios where we face attack and offers practical tactics on wielding the sword of truth, utilizing faith-affirming statements, and standing guard in prayer. I cannot recommend this book highly enough! This beautifully written, hands-on tool against spiritual warfare has rightfully earned a permanent place on my nightstand.

—Donna Snow, speaker and author of *Chosen: A Study of Esther* and
Your Strong Suit: Bible Study on God's Armor

This book is timely, and it is real. No phony or judgmental Christianity included! It's written for real people facing real challenges, especially spiritual warfare. This battle is serious, and the consequences are eternal. With all that is going on in the world, the U.S., the Church, and our lives, its release is a Godsend. The reader will quickly notice the author is a pastor who knows Scripture and the Gospel's power and offers help in understanding the attacks of Satan. The reader is not left to despair in defeat but to delight in the destruction of the devil by the Son of God. You're invited: *Equipped: The Armor of God for Everyday Struggles* is full of fresh insights, honest reflection, meaningful illustrations, and engaging application. Pastor Christopher Kennedy offers great tools and resources for the war-torn Christian that will also be helpful in assisting others in the battles we all face.

—Rev. Dr. Allan Buss, president,
Northern Illinois District, LCMS

EQUIPPED

THE ARMOR OF GOD FOR EVERYDAY STRUGGLES

Christopher M. Kennedy

CONCORDIA PUBLISHING HOUSE • SAINT LOUIS

Published by Concordia Publishing House

3558 S. Jefferson Avenue, St. Louis, MO 63118-3968

1-800-325-3040 • cph.org

Library of Congress Cataloging-in-Publication Data

Names: Kennedy, Christopher M. (Pastor), author.

Title: Equipped : the armor of God for everyday struggles / Christopher M. Kennedy.

Description: St. Louis, MO : Concordia Publishing House, [2021] | Summary: "When we hear the phrase "spiritual warfare," we often think of angels and demons, exorcisms, and demonic encounters. But spiritual warfare also includes the battles we face in everyday life-battles of temptation, doubt, and anxiety. This book will help Christians, especially those who are going through times of struggle, to recognize the spiritual roots of their hardships and to fight against the devil's schemes in the only way that works-with the weapons God gives us in Christ. Both instructional and devotional, each chapter focuses on a piece of the armor of God (Ephesians 6) and how we are equipped in Christ to resist the evil one in our everyday lives. With God's help, readers will find healing, understanding, and peace"-- Provided by publisher.

Identifiers: LCCN 2020036374 (print) | LCCN 2020036375 (ebook) | ISBN 9780758669360 (paperback) | ISBN 9780758669377 (ebook)

Subjects: LCSH: Spiritual warfare--Biblical teaching. | Bible. Ephesians, VI, 11-18--Criticism, interpretation, etc.

Classification: LCC BS2545.S67 K46 2021 (print) | LCC BS2545.S67 (ebook) | DDC 235/.4--dc23

LC record available at https://lccn.loc.gov/2020036374

LC ebook record available at https://lccn.loc.gov/2020036375

3   4   5   6   7   8   9   10   11   12   30   29   28   27   26   25   24   23   22   21

CONTENTS

This book is dedicated with love to my firstborn, Caleb. Caleb, you are a natural leader. The devil works the hardest where he stands to lose the most, and so he targets Christian leaders. Stand strong with the armor of God wrapped around you. You belong to Jesus. As you grow up, you will face challenges. God will be with you, and your mom and dad will always be in your corner, fighting for you with prayer and love.

Finally, be strong in the Lord and in the strength of His might. Put on the whole armor of God, that you may be able to stand against the schemes of the devil. For we do not wrestle against flesh and blood, but against the rulers, against the authorities, against the cosmic powers over this present darkness, against the spiritual forces of evil in the heavenly places. Therefore **take up the whole armor of God**, *that you may be able to withstand in the evil day, and having done all, to stand firm. Stand therefore, having fastened on the belt of truth, and having put on the breastplate of righteousness, and, as shoes for your feet, having put on the readiness given by the gospel of peace. In all circumstances take up the shield of faith, with which you can extinguish all the flaming darts of the evil one; and take the helmet of salvation, and the sword of the Spirit, which is the word of God, praying at all times in the Spirit, with all prayer and supplication.*

To that end, keep alert with all perseverance, making supplication for all the saints, and also for me, that words may be given to me in opening my mouth boldly to proclaim the mystery of the gospel, for which I am an ambassador in chains, that I may declare it boldly, as I ought to speak.

EPHESIANS 6:10–20 (EMPHASIS ADDED)

FOREWORD

For we do not wrestle against flesh and blood, but against the rulers, against the authorities, against the cosmic powers over this present darkness, against the spiritual forces of evil in the heavenly places.

Ephesians 6:12

Our battle is not against flesh and blood. God warns us. He gives us a heads-up. Why do we forget so easily?

When worry fills your mind, when illness strikes you or your loved ones, when confusion tangles your home or schedule, when hopelessness grips your heart, when frustration simmers in your soul, when disasters strike the world, when temptation tears at your willpower, and when trial begins to crush you, it is easy to forget the real battle.

Caught off guard, you get pulled in, eaten up, overtaken, and overwhelmed instead of recognizing the sneaky, roaring lion who prowls around, seeking someone to devour (1 Peter 5:8).

That is why this book is so important. The devil's schemes are not surprising mysteries. God's Word clearly states that we are not unaware of the evil one's ploys (2 Corinthians 2:11). But the distraction and noise of life—as well as our own fallen nature—lull us into forgetfulness.

This book is a critical reminder that there is more to your struggle than meets the eye. You are not merely fighting frustration, feelings, people, traffic, malfunctioning appliances, tragedy, or pain. Spiritual forces are at work to remove your hope in Jesus. The devil wants to demoralize and destroy you. He's desperate. He's been beaten by the crucified Savior, and he knows his time is short (Revelation 12:12).

But you are not helpless, and you are not alone. In this book, Chris Kennedy presents the armor God provides for the battle you face. This battle wear is not locked in a castle somewhere high on a mountain. It is not attire for a privileged few. This is God's armor. It is armor accessible to all. It is Savior-tested protection that Jesus gives by grace (Isaiah 59:17).

Read this book to become armed for the most important battle of your life. Your Savior marches ahead of you—and He outfits you for victory.

Rev. Michael W. Newman
President, Texas District,
The Lutheran Church—Missouri Synod
Author of *Satan's Lies*, *The Great Deceiver*, and
Hope When Your Heart Breaks

PREFACE

For though we walk in the flesh, we are not waging war according to the flesh. For the weapons of our warfare are not of the flesh but have divine power to destroy strongholds. We destroy arguments and every lofty opinion raised against the knowledge of God, and take every thought captive to obey Christ.

2 CORINTHIANS 10:3–5

This book comes out of my experience in spiritual warfare.

I used to think the idea of spiritual warfare was overblown—until I went through my own season of internal torment.

I didn't recognize it as spiritual warfare at the time. As a result, my spirit suffered tremendously. On the outside, it may have looked like I was doing fine. But inside, I was falling apart. My soul was under direct attack, and it took a toll on me.

For about three years, nearly every hour of every day, my mind was haunted by traumatic memories, distortions of truth, and lies about myself that I had accepted as reality.

By God's grace, the dark cloud eventually lifted. God is able to work all things for good (Romans 8:28). He preserved me. And in the crucible of suffering, He molded me into a stronger, wiser, more prepared servant of the Gospel.

Spiritual warfare is real. A war rages within each of us. By God's grace, you don't have to fall prey to the devil's tactics. You can win in spiritual warfare when you are armed with the weapons God provides.

Through my season of struggle, I learned the value of God's weapons— namely, Scripture and prayer. I was weakest when relying too much on human reason and strength. I was strongest when leaning on the divine perspective and power that are accessible to every Christian.

In 2 Corinthians 10, Paul warns us that we're not waging warfare according to the flesh. Our warfare is spiritual, and therefore spiritual weapons are necessary to achieve victory. Satan wants to establish strongholds in our minds and hearts. But if you're a Christian, your mind and heart belong to Jesus, and the devil has no rightful claim to what is God's.

If you're going through a season of struggle right now, I pray that you never lose sight of God's love for you. He remembers you. He will not abandon you, even at your lowest moment. My hope is that this book will give you the tools to overcome by pointing you to God's Word and His strength. Some of those tools are included in the Storehouse of Spiritual Weaponry section, which is a topical collection of Scripture references and other resources related to spiritual warfare. I encourage you to use the Storehouse of Spiritual Weaponry as a go-to resource in times of testing.

This book also is a preemptive measure. As you study what God's Word says about spiritual warfare, you're gathering up the armor you'll need when the day of testing comes. By God's grace, you'll be ready to fight the good fight of faith. And with God's help, you'll come out on top.

Christopher M. Kennedy
San Antonio, Texas
June 2019

UNMASKING
THE ENEMY

*Put on the whole armor of God, that you may be
able to stand against the schemes of the devil.*

EPHESIANS 6:11

*Humble yourselves, therefore, under the mighty hand of God
so that at the proper time He may exalt you, casting all
your anxieties on Him, because He cares for you. Be sober-
minded; be watchful. Your adversary the devil prowls around
like a roaring lion, seeking someone to devour. Resist him,
firm in your faith, knowing that the same kinds of suffering
are being experienced by your brotherhood throughout the
world. And after you have suffered a little while, the God of
all grace, who has called you to His eternal glory in Christ,
will Himself restore, confirm, strengthen, and establish
you. To Him be the dominion forever and ever. Amen.*

1 PETER 5:6–11

One day, after teaching junior high religion class in my church's Day
School, I noticed several students pulling out a book for their next class.
The book was *The Day the President Was Shot*, about the JFK assassination.
I've always been intrigued by President Kennedy. After all, we share the
same last name. (No relation though.) I visited with the teacher about the
book. She suggested I read it. So I did. It was a quick read and an interesting refresher on one of the most shocking events in our nation's history.

A few months later, a family member gave me a book about conspiracy theories surrounding the murder of President Kennedy. It, too, added to my understanding of the complexities surrounding the shooting.

Though the assassination took place more than fifty years ago, both books were written fairly recently. Even after all these years, the debate is still alive: Did the assassin Lee Harvey Oswald act alone? Was he part of a larger plot? Who was really behind the tragic act?

The 1991 movie *JFK* portrays an elaborate web of conspiracy that involved government agencies like the CIA and FBI, both pro- and anti-Castro forces, the Pentagon, Vice President Lyndon B. Johnson, and the KGB. So, what's the truth? Was a larger force behind the murder of a president?

A similar question can be asked for all the evil in our world: who's behind it?

According to the Bible, our battle is not against flesh and blood but against forces of evil. Behind evil acts are evil spiritual influences. Those evil influences not only produce violence; evil forces are assaulting all of humanity every day. You and I are caught in the middle of a war between good and evil *every day*.

Origin of the Evil One

As we begin our study on spiritual warfare by examining Ephesians 6, the passage about the armor of God, let's start with a definition. What is spiritual warfare? What's the difference between having a bad day and being under spiritual attack? Simply put, spiritual warfare is the battle over your spirit. Spiritual warfare is recognizing that there is an ongoing fight between good and evil, and *you* are the prize.

Leading the charge against us is a personal being—the devil, or Satan. Listen to this description of him from 1 Peter 5:8: "Your adversary the devil prowls around like a roaring lion, seeking someone to devour." The devil is hungry for trouble. He craves human souls. More than anything, he wants to pull us away from God. He opposes God and the object of God's affection, people.

According to a widely accepted understanding of certain passages in the Old and New Testaments, Satan is a fallen angel. Originally named Lucifer, he once was in God's inner circle of angels. A passage in Ezekiel 28 addresses the king of Tyre, one of the nations near ancient Israel. Many believe this passage also alludes to Satan in its descriptive poetry:

> **Thus says the Lord GOD: "You were the signet of perfection, full of wisdom and perfect in beauty. You were in Eden, the garden of God. . . . You were blameless in your ways from the day you were created, till unrighteousness was found in you. In the abundance of your trade you were filled with violence in your midst, and you sinned; so I cast you as a profane thing from the mountain of God, and I destroyed you, O guardian cherub, from the midst of the stones of fire. Your heart was proud because of your beauty; you corrupted your wisdom for the sake of your splendor. I cast you to the ground." (vv. 12–13, 15–17)**

It appears that Lucifer was among God's greatest angels, perhaps equal in majesty to Michael the archangel or Gabriel, the angel who appeared to Jesus' mother, Mary. Lucifer was at the top of his class, but his pride got the best of him. Apparently, even angels are not immune to becoming prideful. In Lucifer's case, it was a tragic fall.

Isaiah was another Old Testament prophet who wrote about a foreign king in language that is mysterious and cosmic. Isaiah spoke against the king of Babylon, but as with Ezekiel's writings, many people ascribe a deeper meaning to this passage, associating it with Lucifer's fall:[1]

> **How you are fallen from heaven, O Day Star, son of Dawn! How you are cut down to the ground, you who laid the nations low! You said in your**

---

[1] See, for example, the note on Isaiah 14:12 from *The Lutheran Study Bible* (p. 1115): "Jesus may allude to this passage (Lk 10:18; Rv 12:8–9) in describing Satan's fall from heaven."

> heart, "I will ascend to heaven; above the stars of
> God I will set my throne on high; I will sit on the
> mount of assembly in the far reaches of the north;
> I will ascend above the heights of the clouds; I
> will make myself like the Most High." But you are
> brought down to Sheol, to the far reaches of the pit.
> (14:12–15)

Sheol was a term for the realm of the dead. In this case, it could be equated with hell, which became the devil's cursed abode. By asserting himself against God, Lucifer doomed himself.

Jesus Himself described Lucifer's tragic fall from glory. Speaking to His disciples, Jesus said, "I saw Satan fall like lightning from heaven" (Luke 10:18).

You've probably heard the saying that misery loves company. In the case of Lucifer's fall, the statement is particularly true. According to a popular interpretation of Revelation, when the devil was cast down from heaven, he took with him a third of the angels, who became evil spirits. This teaching is based on Revelation 12. The Book of Revelation uses picture language to communicate spiritual truth. In this case, a dragon is described and identified: "And the great dragon was thrown down, that ancient serpent, who is called the devil and Satan, the deceiver of the whole world—he was thrown down to the earth, and his angels were thrown down with him" (v. 9). A few verses earlier, the passage says that the dragon's "tail swept down a third of the stars of heaven and cast them to the earth" (v. 4). These fallen angels now constitute "the cosmic powers over this present darkness, . . . the spiritual forces of evil" that engage in battle against us (Ephesians 6:12).

Ever since his banishment from God's presence, the devil's goal has been to undermine God and contaminate everything that is good. Knowing that human beings are God's most precious creation, Satan targets us. Satan has a methodology for preying upon our spirits. God's Word instructs us: "Put on the whole armor of God, so that you may be able to stand against the schemes of the devil" (Ephesians 6:11). A more literal translation of the Greek for the word *schemes* would be "expert methods." Satan is no amateur. He is intentional, organized, crafty, manipulative, and experienced.

SATAN'S CHIEF STRATEGY: DECEPTION

At the core of Satan's tactics is deception. With his first victims, Adam and Eve, Satan led them to doubt God's Word: "Did God actually say, 'You shall not eat of any tree in the garden'?" (Genesis 3:1). Satan, disguised as a serpent, introduced doubt into the minds of Adam and Eve. Formerly, they trusted God completely. But with Satan's inquiry, they began to question God's Word.

The devil has continued his pattern of deception ever since. Jesus called the devil "the father of lies" (John 8:44). In one place, the Bible says the devil's work is concealed in "false signs and wonders" (2 Thessalonians 2:9). Satan's goal is to lead the entire world astray, one person at a time, one lie at a time.

The devil chooses to deceive because he is out to crush our spirits and pull us away from God. As a created being limited in power, the devil is not directly responsible for every bad thing that happens to you. He doesn't have that kind of authority. But he does leverage every misfortune for his purposes. If you contract an illness, it's not verifiable to say that the devil made you ill. But the devil will use your illness to prey upon your spirit. He'll introduce thoughts into your mind—doubts about your worth, despair that you'll never fully recover. He'll mislead you to think you've done something wrong and your illness is God's punishment. In spiritual warfare, the battle is over your spirit. Physical hardship, financial misfortune, relational difficulties—none of these are Satan's end goal. He capitalizes on these struggles, distorting the way you view your problems, seeking to crush your spirit.

At the other end of the battle is God. Let me be perfectly clear: God and Satan have opposite purposes, but they are *not* equal and opposite beings! God is the infinite Creator. Satan is a limited, created being. God and Satan both want you. God wants you more, and He has the final say in all matters.

OUR JOB: RESIST!

The Bible tells us to take our stand against the devil's schemes (Ephesians 6:11). We're not told to defeat the devil. As the conquering Lord, Jesus has defeated the devil and all forces of evil. Colossians 2:15 says, "He disarmed the rulers and authorities and put them to open shame, by triumphing over them in Him." Satan has been given his eviction notice and he is on his way out, but he's not going out quietly. He's kicking and screaming on the way to eternal banishment. The Book of Revelation says that Satan's doom is sealed. In the end, God will cast the devil into a lake of burning sulfur and eliminate the presence of evil once and for all (20:10).

This side of heaven, we will not escape spiritual warfare. Jesus defeats; we resist. But by God's grace, we *can* resist the devil. We can take our stand against him. This is what the armor of God is all about. God equips us with what we need for the battle: Truth. Righteousness. Peace. Faith. Salvation. Scripture. Prayer.

All of these things Paul links to a piece of armor in Ephesians 6. Do you know where Paul was when he authored the Letter to the Ephesians? Inside a jail cell in Rome—possibly staring at an armor-clad soldier right outside his cell. If anyone was vulnerable to spiritual attack, it was Paul; he was far from home, chained inside a prison, persecuted, not knowing when or if he'd be released.

With eyes of faith, instead of seeing an impossible situation, Paul looked outside his cell and saw an illustration for how God protects and preserves us. Armed with the spiritual armor he would write about, Paul saw things differently. He saw things God's way, not Satan's way. Confidence, not despair, marked his perspective.

In each chapter of this book, we'll analyze a piece of armor. I want you to walk away from this opening chapter with one key truth: through Christ, you *can* stand firm against the devil's schemes; you *can* stand your ground. The devil wants you to believe a lie—that you're overmatched, outnumbered, out of your league. God counteracts the devil's attacks with truth, the truth of His protection over you in Jesus.

One of the most well-known Bible stories is David and Goliath. It's the account of a boy who defeated a giant. By appearances, the boy was outmatched. Stronger men had faced off against Goliath and failed miserably. The difference with David was not his physical strength. The difference was his unshakable trust in God to deliver him, to fight for him. Standing face-to-face with Goliath, David declared, "The battle is the LORD's" (1 Samuel 17:47).

This is our conviction too. The battle of spiritual warfare belongs to the Lord. He equips us for battle. Armed with His gifts, we will take our stand!

Discussion Questions

1. When you hear the phrase "spiritual warfare," what comes to mind?

2. How do you feel, knowing that there is a battle raging, and you are the prize?

3. How did the chapter confirm, challenge, or reshape your views of the devil?

4. Jesus said, "I saw Satan fall like lightning from heaven" (Luke 10:18). The devil's pride was his downfall. In which area of your life are you most tempted toward pride?

5. Jesus called the devil "the father of lies" (John 8:44). Where do you feel the devil is most active in spreading lies right now?

6. Name a struggle in your life. Think of how the devil might try to assign a distorted meaning to your struggle. Now reframe your struggle and describe it from a perspective of faith in God's goodness and purpose.

7. What is the difference between Jesus' role and our role in spiritual warfare? What does it look like for us to resist?

8. Write down goals that you hope to achieve by reading this book. What about spiritual warfare do you want to understand better?

BELT OF TRUTH

Stand therefore, having fastened on the belt of truth.

EPHESIANS 6:14

Rejoice in the Lord always; again I will say, rejoice. Let your reasonableness be known to everyone. The Lord is at hand; do not be anxious about anything, but in everything by prayer and supplication with thanksgiving let your requests be made known to God. And the peace of God, which surpasses all understanding, will guard your hearts and your minds in Christ Jesus. Finally, brothers, whatever is true, whatever is honorable, whatever is just, whatever is pure, whatever is lovely, whatever is commendable, if there is any excellence, if there is anything worthy of praise, think about these things. What you have learned and received and heard and seen in me—practice these things, and the God of peace will be with you.

PHILIPPIANS 4:4–9

Every year, the Oxford English Dictionary announces its Word of the Year. Winners are words that come into prominence during the year. In 2005, it was *podcast*. In 2007, it was *locavore*, a person who prefers to eat food grown locally. For 2009, they chose *unfriend*, the action of deleting someone from your network of friends on social media. In 2013, *selfie*. And in 2016, the word was *post-truth*.[2]

Some say we live in a post-truth culture. In a post-truth culture, emotion rules and facts are optional. Social commentators attribute the post-truth culture to a combination of the twenty-four-hour news cycle, imbalance in news reporting, and the rise of social media. Reflecting on the Word of the Year, a *Washington Post* article pronounced that truth was dead.[3]

Let's fact-check that statement. Is truth really dead? Not according to God's Word. The words *true* and *truth* appear in the Bible more than 250 times. Jesus spoke of truth often. One time, He said, "If you abide in My word, you are truly My disciples, and you will know the truth, and the truth will set you free" (John 8:31–32). Jesus declared that truth is real, and so we reject the statement that truth is dead. Truth is alive because the risen Lord Jesus is alive. He is the way, the truth, and the life (John 14:6).

Unfortunately, because truth is alive, so is its opposite—lies. In the previous chapter, we discovered that the devil's main tactic is deception. Satan twists the truth. He offers counterfeit truth and seeks to lead the world astray. He introduces doubts into our minds. He distorts how we see ourselves. He does everything he can to undermine God's good work in our lives. By assaulting us with lies, Satan attempts to crush our spirit.

Fasten Your Belt

For that reason, the first piece of armor God gives us is the belt of truth. For my fellow Texans, this should be one of our favorite pieces of armor. We just need to add a big buckle to it! For Roman soldiers, the belt was much larger than the belts we fasten around our waists. Their belts did much more than keep their pants up. Some translations render the word "girdle." The belt could cover a soldier's abdominal area, providing protection there. It also could have straps of leather hanging from it.

---

2   "Word of the Year," Oxford University Press, accessed August 12, 2019, https://languages
     .oup.com/word-of-the-year/.

3   Amy B. Wang, "'Post-truth' named 2016 word of the year by Oxford Dictionaries,"
     Washington Post, November 16, 2016, https://www.washingtonpost.com/news/the-fix
     /wp/2016/11/16/post-truth-named-2016-word-of-the-year-by-oxford-dictionaries/.

Why did Paul choose a belt for truth? A couple of speculations intrigued me. First, if the belt functioned as a girdle covering the abdominal area, it was covering the organs that process and filter food. The truth of God's Word is how we filter what is true from what is not. On the night of His betrayal, Jesus prayed that His followers would stay close to the truth of God's Word. "Sanctify them in truth; Your word is truth," He prayed to His heavenly Father (John 17:17). The most reliable way to separate truth from lies is to filter information through God's Word. A good question to ask is, "Does the Bible have something to say about this?" When the words of people contradict God's Word, you know which to follow.

A second intriguing theory about why truth is a belt has to do with the leather straps that in many cases were attached to the belt. Leather straps hanging down can remind us that Satan likes to hit below the belt. He searches for our weaknesses, where we're most vulnerable. He delivers low blows, hitting us in areas of our lives we'd prefer to keep covered up. He brings to mind our failures. He convinces us that our shortcomings define us. He points out our inadequacies and breeds insecurity in us.

THE PROBLEM OF SELF-DECEIT

With the belt of truth, we reject falsehood. In searching the Bible on the topic of truth, I expected to find a number of verses about the devil's lies. I found several. In John 8:44, Jesus calls the devil "the father of lies." Jesus said that when the devil lies, he's speaking his native tongue. Satan is fluent in lies.

So yes, the Bible does clearly associate lies with Satan. But to my surprise, the Bible links falsehood with someone else in more instances. Do you know who?

Us!

More often than warning against the devil's lies, the Bible cautions against self-deceit!

- **"I said in my alarm, 'All mankind are liars'"**
  (Psalm 116:11).

- "The heart is deceitful above all things, and desperately sick; who can understand it?" (Jeremiah 17:9).

- "No one does good, not even one." "Their throat is an open grave; they use their tongues to deceive" (Romans 3:12–13).

- "If anyone thinks he is something when he is nothing, he deceives himself" (Galatians 6:3).

It's a bleak picture! But it's honest.

With hearts hardened by sin, we deceive ourselves. We deceive ourselves when we think that bad things shouldn't happen to us because we're good people. We deceive ourselves when we continue destructive behavior by saying, "A little more won't hurt," or, "One more time won't do any harm. No one will know." We deceive ourselves when we think that we're always right and everyone else is wrong. Most critically, from 1 John 1:8, "If we say we have no sin, we deceive ourselves, and the truth is not in us." The devil may be the father of lies, but we can be our own worst enemies when we live in self-deception and denial of our problems.

TRUTH PERSONIFIED

In contrast to us, Jesus identified Himself as truth. Standing before Pontius Pilate, Jesus said, "For this purpose I was born and for this purpose I have come into the world—to bear witness to the truth. Everyone who is of the truth listens to My voice" (John 18:37). The way to fight deception is to listen to Jesus. He embodies truth. His word is truth.

Speaking through His holy, inspired Word, Jesus tells us that though we are sinners, He has rescued us by His death on the cross. "He Himself bore our sins in His body on the tree, that we might die to sin and live to righteousness. By His wounds you have been healed" (1 Peter 2:24). More than anything else, God wants us to believe the truth of salvation in Jesus. Because of His sacrifice, we are eternally secure. Along with His resurrection on the third day, Jesus' work on the cross is the greatest truth of all.

Jesus saved us. And Jesus saves us now. He saved our souls for eternity, and He rescues our spirits from attacks of falsehood. He doesn't abandon us to fend for ourselves against the lies that assault our hearts and minds. Jesus is still in the rescue business. He accomplished our eternal salvation through His death on the cross. By uniting us with Himself through faith, He continues to be the Savior of the redeemed in all things.

As residents of a world broken by sin, all of us are in need of rescue every day. Our spiritual predicament resembles that of the soccer team trapped in a cave in Thailand in 2018. While exploring a cave, the twelve boys and their coach were caught off guard by a flash flood. To escape the rush of water, they had to go deeper into the cave. They remained trapped in the cave without food for more than two weeks, utterly helpless. They could not save themselves.

The rescue became an international event. Two divers finally located the missing boys and coach. Bringing them safely out of the cave—nearly four miles round trip—would require seemingly impossible logistics. Some of the boys couldn't swim, and all were severely weakened. The rescue team decided they needed to strap something onto the stranded people to rescue them. Rescue workers designed a rope-and-pulley system. The rope ran from the location where the team was trapped to the opening of the cave. Each boy would be strapped onto a stretcher. Workers spaced throughout the cave operated the pulley system to gradually bring the boys and their coach from the depths of the cave to the light of day.

To rescue us from our helpless spiritual state, God straps something onto us: the belt of truth. We would not pass safely from the darkness of this life to the light of heaven without the truth of Jesus. Furthermore, we'll struggle with the challenges of every day without God's truth in our lives. The belt of truth is an essential part of our deliverance.

Replacing Falsehood with Truth

In spiritual warfare, the battle for truth has two parts. One is rejecting falsehood. The other is replacing it with truth. Leading up to the admonition not to give the devil a foothold, Paul wrote to the Ephesians, "Each of you must put off falsehood and speak truthfully to your neighbor" (4:25 NIV). Put off falsehood. Put on truth.

But it's not enough simply to put off falsehood. For every lie we reject, there's always another one waiting to take its place. Or the same lies might boomerang right back into your mind. By itself, casting off something leaves you uncovered and vulnerable to attack.

A major part of Jesus' earthly ministry was driving out demons. He said that when an evil spirit is cast out, it goes away but then wants to come back. And returning to the same person, finding "the house empty, swept, and put in order" (Matthew 12:44), the demon invites his demon friends to join the party (see vv. 43–45). When we reject lies, we don't want to leave ourselves unguarded and vulnerable. For an effective defense, we have to put on something: the belt of truth!

God tells us the things He desires for us to fill our minds with: "Whatever is true, whatever is honorable, whatever is just, whatever is pure, whatever is lovely, whatever is commendable, if there is any excellence, if there is anything worthy of praise, think about these things" (Philippians 4:8). Just as truth is first on the list of the armor of God, truth is listed first in this passage. God wants us, first and foremost, to fill our minds with what is true.

God speaks truth to us in His Word. The best way to fill your mind with truth is to immerse yourself in God's Word. Through daily discipline, you can read, study, memorize, and meditate on Scripture. In the book *The Purpose Driven Life*, Rick Warren wrote, "If you know how to worry, you already know how to meditate [on God's Word]. Worry is focused thinking on something negative. Meditation is doing the same thing, only focusing on God's Word instead of your problem."[4] If you know how to worry, you know how to meditate on God's Word. Same process, different content.

In the battle over your spirit, you can stand your ground armed with the belt of truth. Truth is found in Jesus and His Word. Truth about who He is. Truth about who you are in Him. Instead of being defined by the

---

4   Rick Warren, *The Purpose Driven Life*, 190.

culture or other people or Satan's lies or our own self-deceptions, you can see who you really are through the lens of Scripture. You are

- **God's child (1 John 3:1),**

- **saved (Ephesians 2:8),**

- **loved (John 3:16),**

- **cherished (Psalm 139:13–16),**

- **protected (Psalm 32:7),**

- **armed (2 Corinthians 10:4),**

- **strong (2 Corinthians 12:9–10), and**

- **ready for battle!**

DISCUSSION QUESTIONS

1. Have your emotions ever clouded your ability to recognize truth? Explain.

2. What do you think Jesus meant when He said, "The truth will set you free" (John 8:32)? How does truth liberate?

3. Why do you suppose the Bible warns against self-deceit more than the devil's deceitfulness?

4. What do you think is the most prevalent type of self-deception?

5. "Along with His resurrection on the third day, Jesus' work on the cross is the greatest truth of all." How would you explain the significance of this statement to someone who knows very little about Christ?

6. Read Philippians 4:8. The verse tells us what kinds of things to think about. Choose two or three words from the list and give concrete examples to match those words.

7. What worries you? What does God want you to do with your worry?

8. Name three truths about who you are in God's eyes.

BREASTPLATE OF RIGHTEOUSNESS

And having put on the breastplate of righteousness.

EPHESIANS 6:14

But now the righteousness of God has been manifested apart from the law, although the Law and the Prophets bear witness to it—the righteousness of God through faith in Jesus Christ for all who believe. For there is no distinction: for all have sinned and fall short of the glory of God, and are justified by His grace as a gift, through the redemption that is in Christ Jesus, whom God put forward as a propitiation by His blood, to be received by faith. This was to show God's righteousness, because in His divine forbearance He had passed over former sins. It was to show His righteousness at the present time, so that He might be just and the justifier of the one who has faith in Jesus. Then what becomes of our boasting? It is excluded. By what kind of law? By a law of works? No, but by the law of faith. For we hold that one is justified by faith apart from works of the law.

ROMANS 3:21–28

*B*ang bang bang.

It was the sound that reverberated through a small university town in Germany. It's the sound that has echoed through more than five hundred years of history. On October 31, 1517, Martin Luther posted a series of ninety-five statements on a church door in Wittenberg, Germany. His teachings on the Gospel sparked a movement known as the Reformation. At the center of the Reformation movement is the scriptural conviction that we're made righteous—or right with God—by grace through faith in Christ alone.

Before Luther was hammering theological statements on a door, he was pounding on himself. Literally. It would be an understatement to say Luther was hard on himself during his years as a monk. He was known to flog himself to try to overcome his carnal impulses, as if he could beat sin out of himself. He would spend hours a day confessing his sins to a priest until the priest could handle no more. Luther, a former law school student, envisioned God as a harsh judge waiting to catch people sinning so He could punish them. Luther figured that if he could reduce his sins, or at least confess all of them adequately, he could avoid harsher divine punishment.

Bang bang bang.

Turning from Guilt to Grace

Ever pounded on yourself? I hope not physically. But I suspect we all have been hard on ourselves. Luther felt like he could never do enough. He couldn't do enough good things. He couldn't express enough remorse for his sinfulness. Perhaps you can relate to feeling guilty over not doing enough. If you have a parent in a nursing home, you might feel guilty that you don't visit or call enough. If you're a parent with children at home, you might feel guilty that you missed an event, that you don't have your child in enough activities, or that you haven't done enough to help your child get ahead in school. If a project doesn't turn out well at work, you might blame yourself, saying, "I should have put in more hours," or, "I should have supervised more closely." Any of us can be burdened by our conscience, feeling we haven't done enough.

Similarly, many people feel inadequate in their relationship with God. When tragedy strikes, you may wonder if you suffered because you weren't devoted enough or sincere enough in your faith. When a loved one falls ill or dies, you may wonder if you could have changed things by praying more. We can worry that personal hardship is a manifestation of God's displeasure. The bottom-line feeling is "I haven't done enough." When feelings of guilt weigh down our hearts—*bang bang bang*—it's like we're pounding on ourselves.

For Luther, the turning point from guilt to grace came by reading, understanding, and believing God's Word. The key passage was Romans 1:17: "The righteous shall live by faith." Through Scripture, Luther discovered that a good relationship with God was a gift received by faith, not by being hard on himself. As Luther read deeper into Romans, he encountered passages like this one: "The righteousness of God has been manifested . . . through faith in Jesus Christ for all who believe. For there is no distinction: for all have sinned and fall short of the glory of God, and are justified by His grace as a gift, through the redemption that is in Christ Jesus" (Romans 3:21–24).

Luther described this righteousness as an alien righteousness, something totally outside of him. Once the Gospel message clicked in his mind and heart, Luther declared, "I felt that I was altogether born again and had entered paradise itself through open gates."[5] With his mind fixed on Jesus, Luther's heart was set free from the overwhelming guilt that had oppressed him.

It is the truth above all truths: salvation is all about Jesus. Our relief from guilt comes from a Savior who suffered in our place, a Savior who felt the pounding of a hammer driving nails through His hands into a wooden cross.

On the cross, He took the punishment we deserved. *Bang bang bang.*

Our guilt. *Bang bang bang.*

Our shame. *Bang bang bang.*

All of it was laid on Jesus: "He is the propitiation [atoning sacrifice] for our sins, and not for ours only but also for the sins of the whole world" (1 John 2:2). Our righteousness is found in Christ alone.

---

5   *Luther's Works* 34:337.

Protecting What Is Vital

God invites us to put on the breastplate of righteousness so that we can find comfort in Jesus. In the preceding chapter, we talked about how the belt of truth affects our eternity and our everyday lives. By the truth of the Gospel, we're saved for eternity, and by God's truth, we're also rescued from the daily lies and temptations the devil throws at us. Similarly, God's gift of righteousness changes our eternity and also affects our everyday experience.

With the connection to a breastplate, Paul shows the centrality of righteousness in the Christian faith. The breastplate was an integral part of a soldier's armor. It protected the torso, which contains vital organs like the heart and lungs. Soldiers wore a breastplate because anything could happen in the field of battle. While a soldier could raise a shield to ward off enemy blows, an attack could come from any angle. The breastplate provided protection against attacks from unexpected directions.

A story in 1 Kings 22 proves the importance of the breastplate. King Ahab of Israel was wounded in battle because of a gap in his armor, an opening that his breastplate should have covered. The king was mortally injured when a soldier "drew his bow at random and struck the king of Israel between the scale armor and the breastplate" (v. 34). The king lacked the protection he needed in a critical area. As a result, he didn't survive the enemy's attack.

In spiritual warfare, we don't want any gaps in our armor. Therefore, it's wise to have a comprehensive understanding of what righteousness is all about. The more deeply we grasp God's truth, the more firmly we can cling to it in time of need.

Theologians make a distinction between imputed and imparted righteousness. *Impute* isn't a word we use a lot in common conversation. It means "to assign or ascribe a quality of one person to another." The only person ever to be perfectly righteous is Jesus. God's Word teaches us that Jesus was "without sin" (Hebrews 4:15). When Jesus died on the cross, He paid the price for our sins. He took on our sinful status and gave us His perfect record. His righteousness is imputed to us as a gift received by faith. Imputed righteousness, then, refers to our eternal salvation. In that respect, righteousness in Christ is the greatest comfort of all.

The other kind of righteousness is imparted righteousness. This refers to how Christ daily works in us to live for Him. Those who believe in Jesus have the Holy Spirit within them, enabling them to do good things: "For it is God who works in you, both to will and to work for His good pleasure" (Philippians 2:13). Imparted righteousness, too, is a great comfort! It means that God arms us with the breastplate of righteousness, helping us in our daily decisions and actions.

THE SUBTLE TRAP OF SELF-RIGHTEOUSNESS

The breastplate of righteousness also serves to protect our hearts from falling into a slippery trap: self-righteousness. When we remember that our righteousness comes from Christ, we are acknowledging that our righteousness does not come from ourselves. Sometimes, people will be turned off to Christianity because they feel that Christians are self-righteous. These outsiders may have experienced Christians looking down their noses, putting on airs, or giving the impression that they're better than others.

A study by the Barna Group wanted to answer the question of whether Christians today act more like Jesus or the Pharisees. The Pharisees were antagonists toward Jesus during His earthly life. They were known for being hypocritical and judging others (see Matthew 23:1–36). For the study, researchers had a list of ten statements that described the actions and attitudes of Jesus and ten statements that described the actions and attitudes of the Pharisees as exhibited in the Gospels. Barna posed these statements to self-identified Christians and asked them whether they agreed or disagreed. Based on respondents' agreement or disagreement with the various statements, the Barna study indicated that

- **51 percent of respondents were mostly pharisaical in both attitude and actions (that is, they were focused on self** and resistant to empathy, love, and sharing their faith with others);

- 14 percent were Christlike in both attitude and actions; and

- 35 percent were either Christlike in attitude or in actions, but not both.[6]

Essentially, more than half of the Christians in the study showed some disconnect between Christlike characteristics and their own actions and attitudes.

Ouch.

Personally, most of the Christians I hang around are kind, humble, unpretentious people. But if we're not careful, any of us can fall into self-righteousness. Pride lurks in every human heart. When we let our guard down, the devil does his mischief in our hearts. Satan would love for us to think we're better than others. He'd love for us to live in the illusion that our decisions are infallible. He'd be thrilled if we measured our goodness based on our own performance instead of the perfect work of Jesus.

A more accurate verdict of our virtue is found in Isaiah 64:6: "All of us have become like one who is unclean, and all our righteous acts are like filthy rags" (NIV). Even our best efforts don't measure up to God's high standards. That's why we rely on the righteousness of Jesus. Anything less is self-deception.

The Gift of True Righteousness

The good news is that we are forgiven. In Jesus, there is full and free forgiveness, and that is the basis for our righteousness. The bad news is that we don't always feel forgiven. God is better at forgiving us than we are at forgiving ourselves. No matter how strong the feeling may be that

---

6   "Christians: More Like Jesus or Pharisees?" Barna Group, June 3, 2013, https://www.barna.com/research/christians-more-like-jesus-or-pharisees/.

God does not forgive us, that feeling does not come from God. It's a feeling that we experience as part of the war raging within us.

The spiritual warfare revolving around our righteousness is presented compellingly in a story from the Old Testament Book of Zechariah. In a scene resembling a courtroom, Satan stood accusing the high priest Joshua of his sins. Joshua was dressed in filthy clothes. His clothes remind us of the filthy rags that adorn our souls because of our sins.

The angel of the Lord spoke up in Joshua's defense: "Take off his filthy clothes." Then the angel, speaking with God's authority, said to Joshua, "See, I have taken away your sin, and I will put fine garments on you" (3:4 NIV).

Instead of filthy garments, Joshua was given rich garments. Instead of the filth of our sin, God covers us in the breastplate of righteousness. God protects us from Satan's attacks by arming us with the assurance that He declares us righteous in His sight because of Jesus.

God's gracious gift is at the heart of the Christian faith: "the righteousness of God through faith in Jesus Christ for all who believe" (Romans 3:22). God places this gift over our hearts with His armor.

I served my seminary internship, called a vicarage, at a wonderful congregation called Christ the King Lutheran Church in Kingwood, Texas, in the Houston area. One of the memories etched in my mind from that year was the Good Friday service. The associate pastor, Doyle Theimer, had spent hours the day before constructing an apparatus to illustrate his sermon. He had a giant wooden cross with a scale hanging from each side, like the scales of justice.

At the end of the sermon, he placed a giant rock on one of the scales, dropping the scale as low as it could go. Then he invited the congregation to come forward and take a pebble from a tray. We each came forward, took a pebble, and placed it on the other scale. Pebble after pebble filled the scale—not with a loud *bang bang bang* but with a light *clink clink clink*—as person after person added their pebbles.

Even with all of the pebbles on the scale, it never budged. The rock was much heavier than the combined weight of the pebbles.

The rock represented Christ's righteousness. The pebbles represented our sinfulness, or unrighteousness. The point was stunningly clear: no matter how much we sinned, our unrighteousness could never outweigh Christ's righteousness.

This is how the Bible says it: "Where sin increased, grace abounded all the more" (Romans 5:20). Chew on that statement for a moment. The more sin there is, the more grace there is. It doesn't make sense, but it's true. God's love fills the universe. It is deeper, higher, wider, and longer than anything we can ever imagine or measure. There is no limit to God's love. And that love covers a multitude of sins—all of our sins.

DISCUSSION QUESTIONS

1. What do you know about Martin Luther? How does it feel to know that an important Christian leader like Luther faced deep spiritual struggles?

2. Why do we have trouble showing ourselves grace? How can we make the shift from guilt to grace?

3. Share your understanding of the word *righteousness*. How does the Christian concept of righteousness give comfort?

4. When people call Christians self-righteous or judgmental, what words or behaviors do they point to as evidence? What might Christians do to prove these labels inaccurate?

5. The Barna study compared pharisaical attitudes and actions to Christlike attitudes and actions. Give an example of Christlike words or behavior you've encountered over the past week.

6. Which do you think is a bigger problem for Christians: guilt or self-righteousness? How about for you? Explain your answers.

7. Pride lurks in every human heart. How do we guard our hearts against pride?

8. How might it change people if they saw their sins as pebbles and Christ's righteousness as an immovable rock that outweighs all sins?

SHOES OF PEACE

*And, as shoes for your feet, having put on the
readiness given by the gospel of peace.*

EPHESIANS 6:15

*These things I have spoken to you while I am still
with you. But the Helper, the Holy Spirit, whom the
Father will send in My name, He will teach you all
things and bring to your remembrance all that I have
said to you. Peace I leave with you; My peace I give to
you. Not as the world gives do I give to you. Let not
your hearts be troubled, neither let them be afraid.*

JOHN 14:25–27

Stress is more dangerous than you might think. Several decades ago, a couple of psychiatrists got together and came up with a rating system to predict what kinds of life stresses were most likely to lead to illness. The tool is called the Social Readjustment Rating Scale.[7] At the top of the list of stressful life changes is the death of a spouse. Number two is divorce. Other stressors I find interesting are major personal injury or illness, retirement, pregnancy, in-law troubles, changing to a new school, and vacation.

Each of these life events is assigned a point value. If the total value of your stressors equals three hundred or more, according to the prediction model, you have an 80 percent chance of a health breakdown in the next two years. Moral of the story: too much stress is bad for you.

---

7   Thomas H. Holmes and Richard H. Rahe, "The Social Readjustment Rating Scale," *Journal of Psychosomatic Research* 11, no. 2 (April 1967): 213–18, https://doi.org/10.1016/0022-3999(67)90010-4.

When we're stressed, we lack peace. We're filled with anxiety. We feel overwhelmed. Our hearts seem to beat faster. We have a hard time shutting off our minds and relaxing. Calm is nowhere to be found when we're under intense stress.

For another category of stress, put yourself in the disciples' shoes toward the end of Jesus' earthly ministry. Jesus had been their teacher and friend for three years. They had placed their hopes in Him, leaving their homes and families to follow Him. Now the end of an era was quickly approaching.

On the evening of His betrayal, Jesus reiterated an announcement shared previously: He would not be with them much longer. "Where I am going you cannot follow Me now, but you will follow afterward" (John 13:36).

Panic set in among the disciples. Jesus was going away? Now? Where? Peter said, "Lord, why can I not follow You now?" (John 13:37). Thomas asked, "Lord, we do not know where You are going. How can we know the way?" (John 14:5).

For Jesus, two departures were looming. One was His death, less than twenty-four hours after speaking the words in our text. He would willingly give His life to pay for our sins on the cross. His followers would grieve because He would be gone—killed and buried in a borrowed grave. Then, after His glorious resurrection and appearance among them for forty days, He would leave again, this time for much, much longer. He would go into heaven to prepare a place for them, He promised (see John 14:2). And in this case, too, they would follow after Him. By faith, they would rejoin their Lord in heaven when their days on earth ended.

Even though Jesus predicted His exit, it still was a stressful event for the disciples. Stress is stress, even if you know it's coming. Parents know children are bound to end up in the emergency room at some point in their upbringing, but when it happens, it's a stressful experience. If you've been in the hospital, you might brace yourself for a hefty bill. Even if you're anticipating it, when you open the envelope and look at the amount due, it's painful to see. As a loved one nears the end of life, you may know it's coming, but the emotional impact can be devastating nonetheless. Grief descends even on those who have tried to prepare themselves emotionally.

All of us will face stressful moments in life. And so Jesus' words are as relevant to us today as they were to His disciples: "Peace I leave with you; My peace I give to you. Not as the world gives do I give to you. Let not your hearts be troubled, neither let them be afraid" (John 14:27).

STEPPING FORWARD WITH PEACE

We never walk alone. In our walking, we're equipped with shoes of peace. You may have to walk through a season of unbearable grief. But you don't walk alone. You may have to trudge through a time of overwhelming pressure. But you don't walk alone. The Lord protects our walking with His shoes of peace.

Shoes may seem like the least important piece of armor. Swords and shields communicate strength to an enemy. Helmets and breastplates demonstrate that the soldiers are ready for battle. But shoes? Who even notices the shoes on a soldier?

The soldier did. He could tell the difference. A soldier could be dressed in the strongest armor possible from head to ankle. But if his feet weren't adequately protected, he was in for trouble. Battles aren't fought on carpet. They are waged on ground covered with debris. Imagine trying to fight while stepping barefoot on jagged rocks, sharp twigs, and irritating pebbles. At the very least, a barefooted soldier would be distracted. At the most, his feet would be cut, bleeding, and in terrible pain.

But with good shoes, a soldier could focus on the battle at hand—on the enemy in front of him, not the ground beneath him. Likewise, when we rely on God's peace, we can focus on what is in front of us, knowing that God Himself supports us as we go forward.

God's peace is different from what the world offers. The world offers a fleeting peace based on circumstances. Temporary peace. Peace when things are going well. A relaxed heart and mind when life is intact and manageable. The problem is that life is rarely intact and manageable. Too often, life feels out of control and unmanageable. In those times, we feel stress, not peace.

Our adversary, the devil, offers peace too. But he's a false peacemaker. The deceiver wants us to believe that welcomed relief comes through numbing methods like abusing alcohol, binge eating, watching addictive images, or impulsive spending. He woos people into religions and cults that promise escape from the stresses of life through spiritual solutions apart from the one true God. Satan tricks us into thinking we've achieved peace when we avoid conflict or compromise our values for the sake of "getting along."

None of those are true peace. They're counterfeits. Sometimes people settle for counterfeit peace. In 1938, Adolf Hitler was displaying overtly aggressive behavior, and the world watched in fear. The Nazi dictator was pressuring Czechoslovakia to give up territory on the German-Czech border. British Prime Minister Neville Chamberlain flew to Munich to meet with Hitler. Along with other foreign leaders, Chamberlain agreed that Germany could have claim to the disputed land, as long as Hitler pushed no farther. Chamberlain's strategy became known as appeasement. Hitler signed a peace treaty. Chamberlain flew back to Britain, proclaiming that the treaty guaranteed "peace for our time."[8]

The next year, Hitler invaded Poland and World War II began. So much for appeasement.

Appeasement is not peace. Numbing is not peace. Avoidance is not peace. Peace is peace.

GOD'S PEACE IS UNIQUE

Jesus says His peace is different from what we could find anywhere else. "My peace I give you," He said. "I do not give as the world gives." His peace is based on eternal truth: God is for you. You never can be truly at peace if you're not at peace with God. St. Augustine, who lived AD 354–430, famously said, "Our hearts are restless until they rest in you."[9]

The peace Jesus gives is transcendent. It doesn't hinge on whether life is smooth sailing. Even when circumstances are turbulent, the peace of Christ remains. It's rooted more deeply than life circumstances. Jesus' peace is a gift of God to everyone who believes in Him.

In his book *Stronger: How Hard Times Reveal God's Greatest Power*, author Clayton King describes a tumultuous season in his life. In a span

---

8   "Munich Agreement," Encyclopaedia Britannica, January 7, 2020, https://www.britannica.com/event/Munich-Agreement.

9   Translated from Augustine, *Confessions* 1:1.

of twelve years, nine close family members died, including both parents, who died within sixteen months of each other. King experienced the depths of grief. And he found support and strength in his faith in Jesus. King asks this question: "Would you rather go through life completely alone and never experience hard times, or would you prefer to go through seasons of difficulty and weakness with someone you loved by your side? I can simplify the question this way: Would you rather have an exemption *from* hard times or a companion *in* hard times?"[10]

Here's the irony of the question: we don't get to choose whether we go through hard times. Life doesn't offer exemptions from pain. But God does offer a Companion. Jesus promised the Companion to His disciples; He promised the Holy Spirit. Depending on the translation, Jesus called the Holy Spirit the Counselor, Helper, Advocate, or Comforter. The Holy Spirit is our Companion. He brings the peace of Christ into our lives because the Spirit gives us faith to believe in Jesus.

We find peace with God only through God's one and only Son. Writing to Gentiles—non-Jews who had joined God's family by faith in Jesus— Paul declared, "Now in Christ Jesus you who once were far off have been brought near by the blood of Christ. For He Himself is our peace" (Ephesians 2:13–14). All of us are far from God by nature. But through Jesus, God brings us near to Himself. Jesus, therefore, is the embodiment, the very definition, of peace.

The Holy Spirit brings us peace by giving us the gift of faith. "No one can say 'Jesus is Lord' except in the Holy Spirit" (1 Corinthians 12:3). The Spirit awakens our heart to know God. Apart from the Spirit's work, we would be doomed to a state of perpetual unrest. By the Spirit's work in our heart, we can know ultimate, lasting peace.

When Jesus informed His disciples that He would be leaving them, He also promised the gift of the Holy Spirit. Our Lord never abandons His people. He always provides what is needed.

---

10   Clayton King, *Stronger: How Hard Times Reveal God's Greatest Power*, 83–84.

Being Ready through the Gospel

Assured that God is for us and with us, we can find peace even when life is anything but peaceful. Listen to this part of the armor-of-God passage again: "As shoes for your feet, . . . put on the *readiness* given by the gospel of peace" (Ephesians 6:15, emphasis added). Armed by God, we are ready for whatever life throws at us.

When we feel angry, we can be ready to find peace by refocusing our hearts on Christ and remembering this: "'Vengeance is Mine, I will repay, says the Lord.' . . . Do not be overcome by evil, but overcome evil with good" (Romans 12:19, 21). When our mind leads us down a path of regret, we can be ready to find peace through letting go of our mistakes, knowing that God forgives our sins through Christ. When our heart is filled with anxiety, we can be ready to find peace through trusting God and knowing all things are in His hands. Dressing us with shoes of peace, God accomplishes what He promises. "The God of peace will soon crush Satan under your feet" (Romans 16:20).

For the record, being at peace doesn't mean we won't feel angry or remorseful or anxious at times. Being a Christian doesn't turn off your feelings. Being a Christian puts your faith ahead of your feelings. The peace of Christ transcends circumstances. It resides deep within us. The bottom-line, bedrock, foundational, immovable fact of your life is that God is for you. All of us feel shaken at times. But *feeling* like a wreck and actually being wrecked is not the same thing. Your foundation holds firm in Christ.

By the grace of God, most of us will go through life with nowhere near the stress that the apostle Paul endured. On two separate occasions, he was almost killed because he was a believer. Once, he was stoned almost to death. Another time, he was almost beaten to death. He was shipwrecked and floated helplessly adrift in the water for two nights. On another occasion, he was bitten by a poisonous snake; people thought he would surely die. One thing after another compounded stress in his life. (You can read Paul's list of struggles in 2 Corinthians 11.) And yet, he was able to make this fabulous confession of faith:

**We are afflicted in every way, but not crushed; per-
plexed, but not driven to despair; persecuted, but
not forsaken; struck down, but not destroyed; always
carrying in the body the death of Jesus, so that the
life of Jesus may also be manifested in our bodies.
(2 Corinthians 4:8–10)**

For some people, like Paul, life can be so very hard. All people endure some degree of hardship. No matter what, God brings His people through just as He did for Paul and for all the saints who have gone before us.

Coming from an opposite angle, if someone were to create a life peace inventory instead of a life stress scale, the life peace inventory could have many items on it. What relaxes you? What brings calm into your life? A day without a schedule? Sitting outside on a beautiful day? Sitting on the couch, watching a movie with family or friends? No matter what is on the list, the top of the life peace scale would be the indwelling of the Holy Spirit. He alone brings a transcendent peace into our lives.

John Newton, author of the hymn "Amazing Grace," once wrote that without the Lord's presence, "a palace would be a prison," but with the Lord, "a prison would be a palace."[11] God's presence is the difference-maker. Christians go through hard times just like anyone else. We're not exempt from pain. But we have a Companion who brings with Him the peace of Christ.

God is with you. Do not let your heart be troubled, and do not be afraid.

---

11   John Newton, "On Grace in the Full Corn," *The Works of Rev. John Newton*, vol. 1, 188.

Discussion Questions

1. If you made a list of the most stressful events in life, what would be on it?

2. What stresses are you facing now?

3. Tell about a time you braced yourself for something stressful. Did your preparations soften the impact?

4. What do you find to be peaceful? It might be a favorite place, a relaxing activity, or something else.

5. Compare the three kinds of peace mentioned in the chapter: the peace offered by the world, the peace offered by the devil, and the peace offered by Christ.

6. Would you rather be exempt from hard times or have a companion in those times? Explain your choice.

7. Name some lies that steal peace. Name some truths that restore peace.

8. Have you ever doubted God's presence? Have you ever felt God's presence? In either or both cases, describe your experience.

SHIELD of FAITH

*In all circumstances take up the shield of faith, with which
you can extinguish all the flaming darts of the evil one.*

EPHESIANS 6:16

*Now Thomas, one of the twelve, called the Twin, was not
with them when Jesus came. So the other disciples told him,
"We have seen the Lord." But he said to them, "Unless I see
in His hands the mark of the nails, and place my finger
into the mark of the nails, and place my hand into His
side, I will never believe." Eight days later, His disciples
were inside again, and Thomas was with them. Although
the doors were locked, Jesus came and stood among them
and said, "Peace be with you." Then He said to Thomas,
"Put your finger here, and see My hands; and put out your
hand, and place it in My side. Do not disbelieve, but believe."
Thomas answered Him, "My Lord and my God!" Jesus
said to him, "Have you believed because you have seen Me?
Blessed are those who have not seen and yet have believed."*

JOHN 20:24–29

We live in a dangerous society. At the church where I serve, we've
been taking proactive measures to protect our congregation and school
families in the event of an act of violence. We pray that the plans never have
to be enacted. But all of us have seen footage and heard reports of deadly
shootings in churches and schools. Preparation can mean the difference
between life and death.

One facet of our safety plan is doors. Which doors have a lock on them and which don't? Which doors should be locked at all times? Which direction does the door open—into the room or outward? Teachers have been instructed on what to do in case of an emergency: lock the doors and do not open them until the crisis has passed.

Doors shield us. We turn the latch to secure the front door at home. We lock the gate to the backyard. Behind the wheel, we make sure car doors are locked. Having a door between us and the outside world provides a barrier of safety.

People have been locking doors for a long time. After Jesus' resurrection, His disciples were thinking about self-preservation. The scene on Easter evening begins like this: "On the evening of that day, the first day of the week, the doors [were] locked where the disciples were for fear of the Jews" (John 20:19a). Of course, they didn't have the same security features we have today; they probably blocked the door with a heavy object or barred it shut. They were afraid that the people who killed Jesus would hurt them too. The disciples felt more secure behind a door than out in the open.

And then something happened. "Jesus came and stood among them" (John 20:19b). The risen Lord came to them. Somehow, He entered the room despite the locked door. For someone who rises from the grave, nothing is impossible!

Jesus' resurrection appearance to His disciples is the second of three stories in John 20 about the risen Lord coming to people in their struggles. First, Jesus appeared to Mary Magdalene outside the empty tomb. Mary Magdalene was filled with excitement, quickly going to the disciples to proclaim the good news. Second, Jesus appeared to the disciples. They "were overjoyed when they saw the Lord" (v. 20 NIV). Third, He came again to the disciples, including one disciple who missed the previous appearance. That disciple was Thomas.

The effect of the third appearance was different from the first two. For Thomas, excitement and joy weren't automatic. Rather than jumping up and down with glee, he questioned whether it really was Jesus standing before him. Ever since, he has been labeled with the unfortunate nickname "Doubting Thomas."

In response to Thomas's hesitation, Jesus showed the doubting disciple His pierced hands and wounded side. Thomas, touching and seeing for himself, confessed boldly, "My Lord and my God!" (v. 28). Ironically, this statement by "the doubter" is the strongest confession of Jesus' divinity of any disciple in the Gospels.

We're told that Thomas was called Didymus, which means "twin." The Bible never says who Thomas's twin is. But I have a hunch who it could be.

It's you.

It's me.

WRESTLING WITH DOUBTS

Perhaps you've wrestled with your own doubts about God or about your faith. You may have doubted God's goodness or His sovereignty or His compassion or that He really cares about you. Often, we experience doubts because of a hardship in life. Pain often leads to doubts. Jesus' death likely had traumatized Thomas and caused him to shut the door to his heart.

Your own traumatic moments may have affected you similarly. In fear, you've barred the door to your heart, determined to prevent anyone from getting close enough to hurt you again. Or you've fantasized about hiding behind a locked door, safe from the potential pain of the outside world. When we've been wounded, we may doubt that God will protect us from future harm. We forget that He is our true shield.

This is spiritual warfare. As discussed earlier in the book, Satan isn't omnipotent. He doesn't have power to do whatever he wants. He's a limited, created being. But he's incredibly resourceful. While he can't cause every kind of calamity, he does leverage our hardships to his advantage. When bad things happen to us, Satan uses those events to introduce doubt in our hearts.

The devil puts forth thoughts like this: If God really loved you, He wouldn't have allowed that to happen. He has forsaken you. You're at the bottom of His priority list. You might as well give up. No use hanging onto futile beliefs.

These sinister suggestions are what the Bible calls "the flaming darts of the evil one" (Ephesians 6:16). In Bible times, fiery arrows were a common weapon used in warfare. The arrows were dipped in pitch and lit. They were a double threat. Not only could the arrows penetrate what they hit, but they could also spread fire among soldiers. Sometimes the arrows were shot directly at an enemy soldier. Sometimes the arrows were aimed to land around the enemy, setting fire to the ground around them and distracting them from their main focus. In a battle, hundreds and even thousands of flaming arrows could be launched into the sky at one time, causing it to feel like fire was falling from heaven.

Similarly, in our moments of trial, when disastrous events shake us personally, Satan sees his opportunity and seizes the moment. He reaches into his quiver, pulls out flaming arrows, and shoots them directly at us. He wants to ignite our doubt and fear into full-blown rejection of Christ.

SHIELDED FROM FLAMING ARROWS

For our defense, God gives us the shield of faith. Not all of the pieces of armor have specific instructions attached to them. This one does: "In all circumstances take up the shield of faith, with which you can extinguish all the flaming darts of the evil one" (Ephesians 6:16). In *all* circumstances. To extinguish *all* the darts.

Many shields in Bible times were specially equipped to combat fiery darts. Some shields were lined with leather or covered in hide and then soaked in water before a battle. When wet, the shield could extinguish flaming arrows.[12] In a similar way, God uses water to protect us from the devil's flaming darts. In Baptism, God clothes us with Christ (Galatians 3:27) and covers us with His grace. Soaking us in the waters of Baptism, God shields us.

Even when facing doubts, a Christian can always look back to God's calling through water and the Word and say, "I am a baptized child of God." Feelings may fluctuate. Circumstances may weaken our resolve temporarily. Hardship may generate questions about our faith. But the

---

12   Thomas M. Winger, *Ephesians* (St. Louis: Concordia Publishing House, 2015), 716.

concrete fact of your Baptism does not change. Your Baptism is a specific moment in time when God promised to be with you in all things. He is faithful to His promise. We can find strength in the knowledge that God's promises do not change.

The presence of our Lord makes all the difference when wrestling with the issues of life. When we are grieving like Mary Magdalene, He comes to us. When we are fearful like the disciples, He comes to us. And when doubts assail us, as they did Thomas, Jesus comes to us. He shields us. He protects us.

It should be said that doubts are natural. We do an injustice to people in their spiritual journey if we judge them for their doubts. People need space to process possibilities, including the possibility of an almighty God. In that space of thought and feeling, the Holy Spirit can operate.

For believers, we have faith in God, but that faith can be shaky at times. If God judged us on the firmness of our faith, we might score well some days, and we might receive failing marks other days. Fortunately for all of us, Jesus said that even small faith—"faith like a grain of mustard seed" (Matthew 17:20)—is sufficient for God to accomplish His work in us. Like all seeds, God wants our faith to grow. By His grace, He increases our faith as we walk with Him.

GOD IS OUR SHIELD

Even more fortunately for us, the shield of faith isn't a mighty weapon because of *our* faith. The shield is effective because of the *object* of our faith. Our shield is God Himself!

> **The word of the LORD came to Abram in a vision: "Fear not, Abram, I am your shield; your reward shall be very great." (Genesis 15:1)**

> **Happy are you, O Israel! Who is like you, a people saved by the LORD, the shield of your help. (Deuteronomy 33:29)**

**The LORD is my rock and my fortress and my
deliverer, my God, my rock, in whom I take
refuge, my shield, and the horn of my salvation.
(2 Samuel 22:2–3)**

When God is in front of us, we are well protected against the fiery darts of the evil one!

STANDING FIRM WITH FELLOW BELIEVERS

And also, what great protection we have when we lock arms with other believers and stand our ground together against Satan. Jesus anticipated others who would join in the fight of faith when He said to Thomas, "Have you believed because you have seen Me? Blessed are those who have not seen and yet have believed" (John 20:29). Blessed are we!

Charles Stanley's description of shields in Bible times is illuminating:

**The Roman shield was made of wood covered with
leather and sometimes with metal. There were two
types of shields. One was small and round; a soldier
wore it on the arm for hand-to-hand combat. The
other type was described as a door . . . [and] covered
most of the soldier's body. . . . When a line of soldiers stood shoulder to shoulder with these shields
in front of them, they created a wall of defense.
Soldiers crouching behind their linked-together
shields could move forward in relative safety and
advance to the front line of battle in unison. The
critical factor was that they stay linked together
without any breaks in the wall created by their
shields.[13]**

---

13   Charles Stanley, *When the Enemy Strikes: The Keys to Winning Your Spiritual Battles*, 159, 161.

Can you guess where I'm going with this point? "Two are better than one" (Ecclesiastes 4:9). When we stand together in faith, we're stronger! When you have fellow brothers and sisters in the Lord cheering you on, supporting you, carrying you when you're weak, and lifting you up, how much stronger you are in your fight of faith!

As the writer to the Hebrews says, "Let us consider how to stir up one another to love and good works, not neglecting to meet together, as is the habit of some, but encouraging one another, and all the more as you see the Day drawing near" (10:24–25). If you don't have a network of Christian friends, I first encourage you to get connected with a local church if you're not already. If you are part of a church, now is the perfect time to get involved.

It was the personal appearance of Christ that convinced Thomas of the resurrection. But don't discount the importance of his fellowship with the other disciples. They prepared Thomas for his encounter with Jesus by telling Thomas what they had seen. And in the years after Jesus ascended into heaven, the fellowship of believers would play an important role for all of the early believers.

Tradition says that Thomas traveled to India and shared the faith there. Indian churches today revere Thomas as their founding father. Consider the miracle of Christ in Thomas's life. He was once hiding with the other disciples behind a locked door. But after Jesus appeared to him, Thomas brought the Gospel boldly to new places. Armed with the shield of faith, he advanced with confidence against the flaming darts of the evil one.

Armed with the shield of faith, you, too, can advance with confidence no matter what darts Satan fires at you. The object of your faith—Jesus—is stronger than the one who attacks your faith. Christ is your impenetrable, indestructible shield!

DISCUSSION QUESTIONS

1. Do you feel the world is becoming more dangerous? How so?

2. What makes you feel safe? unsafe?

3. What are some spiritual doubts you've wrestled with?

4. Describe a time when Satan leveraged a hardship to attack your faith.

5. We do an injustice to people in their spiritual journey if we judge them for their doubts. How do we appropriately give people space for doubts and questions about God?

6. In several places, God is described as a shield. What does it mean to you that God is your shield?

7. Tell about a time when others stood shoulder to shoulder with you and helped you through a struggle.

8. At the end of His conversation with Thomas in John 20, Jesus said, "Blessed are those who have not seen and yet have believed" (v. 29). What do those words mean to you? How do you see yourself in that promise?

HELMET OF SALVATION

And take the helmet of salvation.

EPHESIANS 6:17

You will say in that day: "I will give thanks to You, O LORD,
for though You were angry with me, Your anger turned away,
that You might comfort me. Behold, God is my salvation; I
will trust, and will not be afraid; for the LORD GOD is my
strength and my song, and He has become my salvation."
With joy you will draw water from the wells of salvation.
And you will say in that day: "Give thanks to the LORD, call
upon His name, make known His deeds among the peoples,
proclaim that His name is exalted. Sing praises to the
LORD, for He has done gloriously; let this be made known
in all the earth. Shout, and sing for joy, O inhabitant of
Zion, for great in your midst is the Holy One of Israel."

ISAIAH 12:1–6

The other day, my children pulled their bikes out of the garage. Hanging from each bike is a helmet, including a little pink helmet for my daughter, Emma. I remember during my childhood when it became a law that kids on bikes had to wear helmets. At the time, I resisted. I remember thinking, "Why do I need a helmet?" I recall one time colliding with a friend as we rode bikes. We both went flying through the air. I landed in a neighbor's front yard. Maybe a scrape or two, but no serious injuries. "Why do I need a helmet?"

When it comes to *my* children, however, I want their heads protected! When they grow up and play baseball, I want them wearing a batting helmet. If they play football, they had better wear a helmet. For them, head protection is nonnegotiable.

God wants His children wearing a helmet too. In spiritual warfare, Satan targets our minds. If he gets our minds, he gets all of us. When God protects our minds, He protects our entire being from the devil. The mind is the battleground. Satan attacks through lies, deceptions, trickery, subtle misdirection. Therefore, put on the helmet of salvation!

The good news is that Satan cannot have your mind. Your mind belongs to the Lord because *you* belong to the Lord: "We have the mind of Christ" (1 Corinthians 2:16). Jesus reforms our minds for godly thinking and holy living, as Paul says in Romans 8:6: "The mind governed by the flesh [sinful man] is death, but the mind governed by the Spirit is life and peace" (NIV). By faith in Jesus, yours is the latter: a mind controlled by the Spirit, a mind of life and peace.

SATAN'S FOOTHOLD: DOUBLE-MINDEDNESS

But we have a cunning adversary. Satan knows he can't have your mind. It belongs to God. So the devil tries instead to take a piece of your mind. Not the whole thing. Just a piece. Just a corner. Just a small compartment where he can set up shop. James 1:8 describes a "double-minded man" as "unstable in all his ways." Double-mindedness is the devil's goal; his strategy is that part of you may find security in God, but another part of you is restless, doubting, insecure, anxious, fearful. Call it spiritual schizophrenia. One part believes truth; the other part believes Satan's lies.

Does this dynamic resonate with you? Is there a corner of your mind where Satan has set up shop with his lies?

You might be restless. Satan has convinced you of a lie that who you are isn't good enough, or what you have isn't sufficient.

You might be experiencing doubts. Maybe not doubts about God's existence, but doubts about His love or His forgiveness or His power to help you.

You might feel insecure. We live in an age of comparisons. A study of college students revealed that after spending time on Facebook, students reported feeling considerably less satisfied and more critical of their own lives. We see other people's triumphant postings, and insecurity grows within us.[14]

You might feel anxious or fearful. You think about the future in terms of worst-case scenarios. You get worked into a frenzy over something that hasn't even happened.

None of these thoughts have driven out your faith. Jesus remains sovereign in your heart and mind. He is faithful to His promise: "And this is the will of Him who sent Me, that I should lose nothing of all that He has given Me, but raise it up on the last day" (John 6:39). Jesus never lets go of us. But that doesn't prevent the devil from trying. In our struggles, Satan uses any opening he can find to carve out space to harbor his deceptions.

This is where we most often find ourselves. We remain Christians, but we don't receive the full comfort of our faith because we're being pulled in multiple directions. On the one hand, we have the peace of knowing that Christ forgives and loves us. Yet on the other hand, we struggle to forgive ourselves and others. We experience joy from the many blessings God gives us, but we also worry whether God is going to provide in our deepest struggles. We may want to do God's will in certain areas but not in others. Double-mindedness is spiritual instability, and it's Satan's tactic against us in spiritual warfare.

GUARDING YOUR MIND

With prevailing faith in the Lord, we pray against the devil's schemes. David prayed in Psalm 86:11, "Give me an undivided heart, that I may fear Your name" (NIV). Our prayer is for God to bring every area of our

---

14   Ethan Kross et al., "Facebook Use Predicts Declines in Subjective Well-Being in Young Adults," August 14, 2013, *Plos One*, https://doi.org/10.1371/journal.pone.0069841.

lives into alignment so that we can experience His peace and do His will. We want the peace of Christ to rule every facet of our lives: our home, our friendships, our workplace, our finances, our health. And that's what God wants for us too.

The helmet of salvation is the fifth piece of armor described in Ephesians 6. You're probably familiar with the common image of a Roman soldier's helmet: gold- or silver-colored metal covering the head, and maybe something that looks like a brush on top. Helmets were worn for defense, and some were designed to denote rank and standing. Like a bicycle helmet today, a soldier's helmet also was helpful for protecting the soldier's head if he fell off his horse.

Militaries have always understood the importance of a helmet. It's one of the oldest forms of protection in battle. The ancients understood as we do today: no matter how well the rest of the body is covered, if you sustain a head injury, your ability to fight is compromised at best, or at worst, you're out of the fight altogether. If your brain can't function properly, you can't function properly.

Ephesians 6 is not the only mention of the helmet of salvation in Scripture. The helmet of salvation also is named in 1 Thessalonians 5:8–9: "But since we belong to the day, let us be sober, having put on the breastplate of faith and love, and for a helmet the hope of salvation." In this verse, the helmet is linked with the *hope* of salvation. God desires that we live as hopeful, not hopeless, people. Nothing helps us to live hopefully like the knowledge of our salvation in Jesus.

Reaching back to childhood memories one more time, when I was growing up, I wondered why the pastor preached about Jesus so much. Out of all the great Bible stories, why did he always repeat that Jesus died on the cross and rose from the dead? I understood that. I understood it from last week and the week before. Why did the pastor keep reminding us every week of something he had already taught us thoroughly?

But Jesus' death and resurrection is not one of many Bible stories. It is *the* story. Every other story points to Jesus. All of Scripture points to Jesus. The cross is the ultimate act of salvation. The cross defines God as the God of salvation. The cross casts its shadow and the empty tomb sheds its light backward and forward onto every page of Scripture.

THE GOD OF OUR SALVATION

In Isaiah 12, the prophet celebrates God as the God of salvation. Interestingly, the prophet was not celebrating deliverance that already occurred; it was still to come. Twice in the chapter, the prophet wrote "in that day" (vv. 1, 4). He is celebrating God as the author of salvation who sometimes delivers immediately and other times, in His perfect wisdom, delays until "that day." Regardless of when deliverance comes, Isaiah rejoiced in the timeless characteristic of God as Savior. "Behold, God is my salvation; I will trust, and will not be afraid" (v. 2). He is the saving God who rescues His people and grants safety. The prophet fixes this truth in his mind and yearns to declare it to others: "Make known His deeds among the peoples" (v. 4). "Let this be made known in all the earth" (v. 5). Knowing the God of salvation renews, restores, and gives life.

Therefore, salvation is a helmet. The assurance that God is our Savior guards our minds. In whatever perils we face, we know that the Savior is at work in our lives. The devil wants us to believe that God has abandoned us, at least in some areas of our lives. Not true. Armed with the helmet of salvation, the truth of our salvation resides in the forefront of our minds. We recall our salvation in Christ and know that the God who delivers is by our side.

ABSORBING GOD'S WORD

One way to strap on the helmet of salvation is to memorize Scripture. It may seem old-fashioned to memorize verses, but when you do, you establish them firmly in your mind for instant deployment when under Satan's attack. None of us has the mental capacity to memorize all of Scripture, but I encourage you to choose a few verses related to salvation. Read them over and over. Practice saying them without looking at the words. Commit God's Word to memory, and the helmet of salvation fits itself firmly around your head.

Not sure where to start? Here's a sampling of verses many Christians find comforting.

"Be still, and know that I am God" (Psalm 46:10). Years ago, I surveyed my congregation to ask for their favorite Bible verses. This one was mentioned the most often. Our souls find rest when we slow down, stop fretting, and turn our troubles over to the Lord. Imagine being in a tense situation. In that moment, the Holy Spirit can call to mind these words to settle you down and give you peace that God has your problem under control.

"For I know the plans I have for you, declares the LORD, plans for welfare and not for evil, to give you a future and a hope" (Jeremiah 29:11). These words were written for believers in exile in Babylon hundreds of years before Jesus. We believe that what God spoke to them is true for us too. God has a plan for each of us. More often than not, when I want to encourage someone, I tell them that God has a plan for them. This is how God articulated that message a long time ago, and the words are true for us today.

"My grace is sufficient for you, for My power is made perfect in weakness" (2 Corinthians 12:9). Paul wrote these words from the Lord after pleading with Him to remove his thorn in the flesh. The thorn remained, and Paul learned to rely on God while suffering. God's grace proved sufficient for the apostle. God's grace is enough for us too. This verse is a great one to call to mind when you've reached the limit of your strength and recognize your need for God's strength to carry you.

One more. "And we know that for those who love God all things work together for good, for those who are called according to His purpose" (Romans 8:28). When Satan tries to convince us that we're beyond hope, this verse insists otherwise. Even in the worst messes, God can produce good. Out of the ashes, He can renew us and lead us forward. Nothing is beyond God's ability.

Even better than memorizing individual verses is committing longer sections of Scripture to memory. The passage most Christians can recite by heart is the Lord's Prayer, words originally spoken by Jesus (Matthew 6:9–13). Psalm 23 is another passage many people have memorized, reassuring them that the Lord is our shepherd.

A member of my congregation is the athletic director for a local school district. The district has a policy to keep football players "on their toes" at all times. The policy is that, with rare exceptions, players must keep their helmets on throughout the game, even when on the sidelines. They need to be ready at a moment's notice for the coach to send them into the game.

Absorbing God's Word is keeping your helmet on at all times. Trouble can come at a moment's notice. Armed by the Lord, when the day of trouble comes, you will be ready to take your stand.

Discussion Questions

1. What do you think is a favorite corner of people's minds where Satan tends to set up shop? Where are you most vulnerable to deception and misdirection?

2. On a scale of 1 to 10 (with 1 being "not hopeful at all" and 10 being "extremely hopeful"), how hopeful are you? Do you tend to be more optimistic or pessimistic?

3. Colossians 3:15 tells us, "Let the peace of Christ rule in your hearts." How might the peace of Christ rule more fully in your life? Think about specific areas in your life, such as home, friendships, the workplace, finances, and health.

4. Are you waiting for God's deliverance? What is hard about waiting for "that day"?

5. How can your waiting become more faith filled and productive?

6. What topics do you feel get the most attention in sermons? What would you like to hear more about? Consider sharing your list with your pastor.

7. Have you ever memorized Scripture? Tell about a time when a Bible verse came to mind.

8. Choose one of the sample memory verses from this chapter and explain how it's helpful for you as you live for Christ.

SWORD OF THE SPIRIT

And the sword of the Spirit, which is the word of God.

EPHESIANS 6:17

Then Jesus was led up by the Spirit into the wilderness to be tempted by the devil. And after fasting forty days and forty nights, He was hungry. And the tempter came and said to Him, "If You are the Son of God, command these stones to become loaves of bread." But He answered, "It is written, "'Man shall not live by bread alone, but by every word that comes from the mouth of God.'" Then the devil took Him to the holy city and set Him on the pinnacle of the temple and said to Him, "If You are the Son of God, throw Yourself down, for it is written, "'He will command His angels concerning You,' and "'On their hands they will bear You up, lest You strike Your foot against a stone.'" Jesus said to him, "Again it is written, 'You shall not put the Lord your God to the test.'" Again, the devil took Him to a very high mountain and showed Him all the kingdoms of the world and their glory. And he said to Him, "All these I will give You, if You will fall down and worship me." Then Jesus said to him, "Be gone, Satan! For it is written, 'You shall worship the Lord your God and Him only shall you serve.'" Then the devil left Him, and behold, angels came and were ministering to Him.

MATTHEW 4:1–11

After His Baptism, Jesus was led into the wilderness by the Holy Spirit. There, Jesus fasted forty days and forty nights. Sensing a moment of weakness, the tempter came to Jesus. Hearing Jesus' stomach rumble, the tempter suggested, "If You're the Son of God, tell these stones to become bread." Ignoring His hunger, Jesus shook His head no and refused.

Taking Jesus to the highest point of the temple, the tempter said, "If You're the Son of God, throw Yourself down. Test God's promise in the Psalms to send angels to Your rescue." Looking way down, Jesus quickly ruled out taking the risk and shook His head no.

From the vantage point of a high mountain, the devil showed Jesus the kingdoms of the world and said, "All this I will give to You if You bow down and worship me." The Son of God shook His head no.

How is the story I just told you different from the real events in the Bible? The key difference is that in my pretend version above, Jesus didn't speak against the devil's words. In the *real* version, recorded in Matthew 4, Jesus countered all three temptations with God's Word. In my pretend version, Jesus is passive. He absorbs the devil's blows and resists but never fights back. In the real account, Jesus defeats the devil with God's Word.

Going On the Offense

In the description of the armor of God in Ephesians 6, the final piece is the sword of the Spirit, the Word of God. Out of six pieces of armor, the first five are defensive: belt, breastplate, shoes, shield, and helmet. But the sword is different. It's an offensive weapon. We don't just sit back and take hit after hit from the devil. We fight back. God gives us a weapon to injure the devil, to push him back, to overrun his territory and claim it for God. In spiritual warfare, we fight evil.

One of the great dangers in spiritual warfare is passivity. All of us are guilty of sins of omission. We have the chance to speak out against something wrong and we don't. We don't confront gossip or slander. We have an opportunity to help someone but we don't. In Jesus' parable of the Good Samaritan (Luke 10:25–37), two religious leaders sin against an injured man by sidestepping him and not stopping to help. Marriages suffer not only because husbands and wives say things that hurt each other but also because they fail to say the positive, uplifting words that strengthen marriages. The passive life is not the victorious life that God intends for us.

Jesus fought back against the enemy when tempted in the wilderness. He jabbed the sword of the Spirit directly into the devil. Three times, Jesus stabbed Satan with the sword of God's Word. Three Scripture passages, each specifically refuting the devil's attempts. After being pierced by the sword three times, the devil limped away. Christ was victorious over the devil in the wilderness, previewing His victory over sin, death, and the devil through the cross and empty tomb.

A fighting mentality may feel unusual to us as Christians. After all, the Bible tells us in Romans 12:18 that we should, "as far as it depends on you, live peaceably with all." We know Jesus' words in the Beatitudes: "Blessed are the peacemakers" (Matthew 5:9). Jesus described Himself as "gentle and lowly in heart" (Matthew 11:29). Aren't we supposed to be gentle and lowly in heart? Not fighters, but peacemakers?

With other people, yes. But not when it comes to the devil. We are never to be at peace with him. If you're trying to live peacefully when under attack from the devil, then for all of your noble intentions, you'll get obliterated. The only peace the devil will accept is complete surrender. And that's a price none of us would ever want to pay.

So we have to make the distinction. Yes, we are to be at peace with other people as much as possible. But we're never to be at peace with Satan. Just the opposite! We are to fight him with everything we've got. If you're timid by nature, it's time to develop a fighting spirit when it comes to spiritual warfare.

In spiritual warfare, our daily battle, we are on the offensive. The sword of the Spirit, the Word of God, is our offensive weapon. The Roman soldier's sword was called the *gladius*. The word *gladiator* means "swordsman." The gladius was sharpened on both sides and had a pointed tip capable of piercing armor. Paul demonstrates the assertive power of the sword of the Spirit, the Word of God, when he writes, "For the word of God is living and active, sharper than any two-edged sword, piercing to the division of soul and of spirit, of joints and of marrow, and discerning the thoughts and intentions of the heart" (Hebrews 4:12).

Armed by God, we push back forces of darkness in this world to advance God's kingdom. We are not just on the defense. We go on the offense! One of my favorite passages on spiritual warfare is 2 Corinthians 10:4: "For the weapons of our warfare are not of the flesh but have divine power to destroy strongholds."

OVERTHROWING SATAN'S STRONGHOLDS

The word *stronghold* appears at least fifty times in the Bible. The word commonly refers to a fortress with difficult access. When the devil establishes a stronghold in us, he's setting up a fortress that is hard to penetrate and overcome. We all have them—the old, seemingly insurmountable challenges that we wrestle with but never seem to fully overcome. A quick temper. Weakness against temptation. Filthy language. A habit of making the same bad choices over and over. A judgmental spirit. Deeply ingrained flaws of one kind or another.

While the devil thinks he has insurmountable strongholds in our lives, God has other plans. The Lord arms us to overthrow and destroy what the devil has established. The passage continues, "We destroy arguments and every lofty opinion raised against the knowledge of God, and take every thought captive to obey Christ" (2 Corinthians 10:5). Did you hear those active, power-packed words? We *destroy* lies! We lead our enemy *captive* into the obedience of Christ! We go on the attack against the enemy!

When the devil attacks us with lies, we respond with the truth. Spiritual warfare is the devil's intentional effort to use our struggles to discourage us and make us want to give up. Where the devil has established lies in our minds, we overthrow those strongholds. Where lies have taken residence in our minds, we evict those lies. We take them captive and march them over to Christ. We do not sit back passively against deception. We respond with truth. We fill our minds with truth. We deploy truth for action against the enemy.

WIELDING SCRIPTURE ACCURATELY

In the previous chapter about the helmet of salvation, you read about memorizing God's Word so that it's available in time of need. Jesus didn't have a Bible to open during Satan's onslaught in the wilderness. Jesus recited Scripture from memory in the heat of the battle. He didn't just say to the devil, "That's a lie." He also fought back, saying, "Here's what Scripture says is true!"

Wielding the sword of the Spirit, however, is more than just memorizing isolated Bible verses. In addition to knowing individual verses, it's also important that we know the context and overall message of Scripture. People regularly misuse Bible verses as sound bites, manipulated to mean a variety of things.

Take Matthew 7:7, for example: "Ask, and it will be given to you." This verse has been used as the basis for name-it-and-claim-it theologies. Want a million dollars? Just ask for it, and it's yours! And if you ask and don't receive it, that just means your faith is inadequate.

Really? Is that what the verse means? Or is it actually about trusting in God and looking to Him as the source of every good thing? A deeper, more balanced investigation of the whole of Scripture is the best way to rescue verses from misuse and misunderstanding. As we dig deeper into Scripture, we see a picture of God as a good Father who gives His children what they need but not always what they want. He knows what is best for us.

Too often, people misrepresent Scripture to advance their own agendas. Anyone can quote the Bible. But not everyone quotes it accurately or faithfully. Note that in Jesus' temptation, even the devil quoted Scripture. The devil tried to grab the sword from Jesus' hand and stab our Lord with it. But Jesus deftly reclaimed the sword for its true purpose: to communicate God's will. And God's ultimate will was that Jesus would not stop short of the cross but would complete His mission to rescue fallen humanity by His atoning death.

We wield the sword of the Spirit correctly when we understand that individual verses are supporting the overall theme of Scripture: We are sinners. Christ died to redeem us. By faith in Him, we are God's children. Clothed with Christ, we are victorious.

AUTHORITATIVE SWORDSMANSHIP

Jesus spoke Scripture against the devil with authority because Jesus rightly understood His authority as God's Son. To see how clearly Jesus understood His identity, all we have to do is look at the wider context of the temptation story. Scripture is always best viewed in context.

The account of Jesus' temptation in Matthew 4 begins with a word we often gloss over. *Then*. If you look back at the Bible passage at the beginning of this chapter, you'll see the word. *Then* means this account follows another; there's context for the events. The story right before our text is Jesus' Baptism.

Jesus' Baptism was the beginning of His public ministry. We don't know everything that took place before His Baptism. We know about His birth, the visits of shepherds and Magi, Jesus' dedication in the temple, the Holy Family's escape to Egypt and return to the Holy Land, and Jesus' visit to the temple at age 12. Other than those things, the Bible is silent on Jesus' early life.

At age 30, Jesus entered into the public eye. He approached His relative John the Baptist, who was baptizing in the Jordan River. John tried to deter Jesus, saying that Jesus should be the one performing the Baptism, not the other way around. But Jesus insisted, and John consented.

As soon as Jesus came out of the water, two miracles occurred. First, the Holy Spirit descended on Him in the form of a dove. The Spirit's appearance reinforced the words of Isaiah 11:2: "The Spirit of the LORD shall rest upon Him, the Spirit of wisdom and understanding, the Spirit of counsel and might, the Spirit of knowledge and the fear of the LORD."

The second miracle wasn't visual but auditory. A voice spoke from heaven. God issued His definitive Word: "This is My beloved Son, with whom I am well pleased" (Matthew 3:17). Jesus heard it loud and clear. The Word of God declared Jesus to be the beloved Son of God.

With boldness as God's Son, Jesus fought Satan in the wilderness with the sword of the Spirit, the Word of God. The sword belonged to Jesus because Jesus belonged to His Father.

The sword of the Spirit is not only individual Bible verses that we wield at the devil. The sword is also who God says we are in His Word. The sword is God's life-shaping, identity-forming declaration of who He has made us to be in Christ. As it says in 1 John 3:1, "See what kind of love the Father has given to us, that we should be called children of God; and so we are."

And so we are! Likewise, the sword belongs to you because you belong to God. By faith in Christ, you are God's child. God places the sword of truth in His children's hands. He arms us for battle. We go into battle as victors. We are not losers. We're not playing to tie. We're winners in Christ. We live out our victory as we boldly take our stand against every lie, every deception, every attempt to crush our spirits. We counter lies with truth from God's Word. We stand our ground with confidence as God's children.

DISCUSSION QUESTIONS

1. Hebrews 4:15 states, "For we do not have a high priest who is unable to sympathize with our weaknesses, but one who in every respect has been tempted as we are, yet without sin." What comfort do you find in knowing that Jesus faced temptation just as we do?

2. Have you ever struggled with being too passive? Share as you're comfortable doing so.

3. Do you normally consider yourself a fighter? What makes that term feel natural or unnatural based on your personality?

4. Identify an area in your life in which you need to exhibit more of a fighting spirit.

5. How can you tell whether a Bible verse is being used correctly or is being taken out of context? Can you think of a time when you had to make that distinction?

6. "No temptation has overtaken you that is not common to man. God is faithful, and He will not let you be tempted beyond your ability, but with the temptation He will also provide the way of escape, that you may be able to endure it" (1 Corinthians 10:13). What do you understand this verse to mean?

7. Jesus encountered temptation armed with the truth that He is God's Son. How can your status as God's child help you withstand temptation?

8. We've studied the six pieces that constitute the armor of God. Which piece of the armor do you need most right now? Explain why.

PRAYER WARFARE

*Praying at all times in the Spirit, with
all prayer and supplication.*

EPHESIANS 6:18

*And He came out and went, as was His custom, to the Mount
of Olives, and the disciples followed Him. And when He came
to the place, He said to them, "Pray that you may not enter
into temptation." And He withdrew from them about a stone's
throw, and knelt down and prayed, saying, "Father, if You
are willing, remove this cup from Me. Nevertheless, not My
will, but Yours, be done." And there appeared to Him an
angel from heaven, strengthening Him. And being in agony
He prayed more earnestly; and His sweat became like great
drops of blood falling down to the ground. And when He rose
from prayer, He came to the disciples and found them sleeping
for sorrow, and He said to them, "Why are you sleeping?
Rise and pray that you may not enter into temptation."*

LUKE 22:39–46

My colleague Pastor Doug Bielefeldt really angered the devil. As
the pastor assigned specifically to our Day School, Pastor Doug visited
each of our classrooms on a recent afternoon. School didn't actually start
until the next day, so you might think he got his days mixed up and made
classroom visits a day early. But he went a day early on purpose: to pray

over every classroom. He prayed for the children who would be sitting in the seats and for the teachers who would be teaching them. And the devil cringed at every moment of it.

Satan does not like prayer. He'd rather God's people be anxious, disillusioned, worried, fearful, burdened, burned out, and overwhelmed, trying to do things on our own without God's help. Satan wants us to drift from God. Satan wants us to give up. Prayer is a direct attack on everything the devil desires.

And so Satan does everything in his power to keep us from praying. He convinces us that prayer is futile, or it's awkward, or we're too busy to pray, or we're unqualified to pray. When we get past his first line of defense, when we do pray, he tries to distract us in prayer. He doesn't want us to pray because it interferes with his purposes.

Prayer is spiritual warfare. The armor-of-God passage concludes by saying that we should pray "at all times in the Spirit, with all prayer and supplication" (Ephesians 6:18). All occasions. All kinds of prayers and requests. The word *all* takes away the excuses Satan forces upon us. Any time is a good time to pray. Anything on our minds has a place in our prayers. Jesus is always there, ready to listen to our prayers.

Standing Guard in Prayer

Ephesians 6:18 continues: "With this in mind, be alert and always keep on praying for all the saints" (NIV). Be alert, like a guard standing at attention. On the night of His betrayal, Jesus went into the Garden of Gethsemane. Bringing His disciples with Him, He gave simple instructions: "Pray that you may not enter into temptation" (Luke 22:40). Stand guard in prayer. Did they? No. Luke lets them off easy by describing only one time when Jesus came back and found them asleep. Mark's Gospel reveals it happened three times. The disciples repeatedly failed to be alert in spiritual warfare.

We, too, can fail to stand guard in prayer. God has given us family members and friends in need of prayer. He has given us schools in need of divine protection. He has given us a nation in need of God's guidance and blessing. He has given us a church that is sustained only by God's gracious hand. Do we stand guard in prayer over these things? Jesus appoints us as watchmen—sentries—to do battle against forces of evil. But we, like the disciples, can fall asleep on the job by not praying.

When Jesus returned from praying and found the disciples asleep, He said, "Why are you sleeping? Rise and pray that you may not enter into temptation" (Luke 22:46). His instructions didn't change. The mission didn't change. His love for them didn't change.

His love for them, and for all of us, was shown in how He spent His time in prayer. In anguish, Jesus prayed that the cup of suffering might be taken away from Him, but He completely submitted Himself to the Father's will. Jesus was preparing Himself to die on the cross for disciples who would fall asleep instead of stand guard in prayer for Him. Jesus died for people like you and me who are weak in faith, sporadic in prayer, and prone to fall into temptation.

His love for us doesn't change. He sweat drops of blood in the garden for you and me. He bled on the cross for you and me. He lives again for you and me to hear our prayers and even to pray for us before the throne of our heavenly Father.

In the garden, Jesus and the disciples were engaged in spiritual warfare. The text makes it clear. The disciples fell asleep not because they stayed up too late the night before or because they had too much wine in the Upper Room. They fell asleep exhausted from sorrow. Their spirits were crushed, and so they didn't pray. On the other side of the garden, as Jesus wrestled in prayer, an angel from heaven strengthened Him. A spiritual battle requires spiritual strengthening. Where the disciples faded, God the Father ensured that His Son would not. In that moment, He strengthened Jesus for what? To keep on praying. To keep on fighting the good fight. After the angel came to Him, Jesus did what? He prayed, and with even greater intensity.

PERSEVERING IN PRAYER

Prayer is spiritual warfare. We push back evil through prayer. We frustrate the devil through prayer. Jesus also taught about prayer using the parable of the persistent widow (Luke 18:1–8), a story about a judge and a poor widow. The judge didn't care about anyone. But the widow pestered him relentlessly, asking for justice against her adversary. Eventually, the judge gave in and granted her request. It's a lesson in contrasts. If an unjust, uncaring judge hears a plea and finally does what is right, won't our loving, just God do what is right when His people come to Him in prayer?

The introduction to the parable is revealing in itself: "Then Jesus told them [His disciples] a parable to the effect that they ought always to pray and not lose heart" (Luke 18:1). Prayer is perseverance. The devil wants us to give up. When we pray, we persevere. And when we persevere, we keep praying.

Ephesians 6:18 tells us to be alert and keep praying for all the saints. Prayer warfare is not only prayers for ourselves but also doing battle on behalf of others. People you care about are not just struggling with common issues. They're engaged in spiritual warfare. How encouraging for them to know you're fighting for them in prayer!

Earl Heath was on our shut-in list for a long time. I'd bring Communion to him once a month. One time, he pulled out a binder and opened it. He showed me a list of names. He said, "These are all the pastors I know. I pray for them each by name every day." At the end of the list was my name. I was deeply touched to know Earl was fighting for me in prayer every day.

Couldn't we all use an Earl in our lives? How encouraging it is when you know that someone is fighting for you in prayer!

Pastors and church leaders, the devil doesn't want people to hear the Gospel, and he certainly doesn't want them sharing the Good News of salvation with others. How refreshing it is to find out that church members are fighting for you in prayer.

Husbands and wives, Satan knows that if he can create a wedge in your marriage, he can unravel God's good gift of family. How empowering it is to know that other couples who understand your struggles are fighting for you in prayer.

Moms and dads, the devil recoils at the fact that you're sharing Jesus with your children at a young, impressionable age. He'd rather a secular, godless mindset prevail. How hopeful it is to know that others are praying for you and for your children.

Single people, Satan wants you to feel lonely and discontented with life. How reassuring it is to know that Satan's lies will not prevail because you have a loving support network lifting you up in prayer.

Seniors, the devil wants you to become discouraged by physical ailments and depressed by losses. How uplifting it is to know that you're not forgotten but are in the prayers of your loved ones.

We receive an extra boost of strength when we find out someone is praying for us. And we strengthen others when we tell them that we are praying for them. Don't keep it a secret. Today is the day to pray for others and to let them know they're in your prayers! The simple knowledge that you care enough to pray speaks volumes to them.

Satan would chuckle to himself if God's people talked about prayer but didn't actually pray. Ephesians 6 tells us the armor of God is ours so we can make our stand against the devil. In that spirit, let's close the chapter with a prayer:

> **Dear heavenly Father, we stand by Your power and grace. We intercede for pastors and ministry leaders. Protect them and their families from Satan's attacks. We lift up all Christian families. Protect marriages. Guard the hearts and minds of children. Grant that all individuals at every stage of life would know of Your presence and purpose for them. Expose Satan's lies. Cast out deception from among us and within us. Replace it with Your truth. We ask these things boldly, confidently, in the name of Jesus, who is the way, the truth, and the life. Amen.**

DISCUSSION QUESTIONS

1. On a scale of 1 to 10 (with 1 being "weak" and 10 being "strong"), how would you rate your prayer life?

2. When do you normally pray during the day? Describe any routines or disciplines you have related to prayer.

3. What do you think are the most common excuses not to pray?

4. In the Garden of Gethsemane, the disciples failed to pray because they were exhausted from sorrow. What exhausts you? What replenishes you?

5. In the Garden of Gethsemane, angels attended Jesus to strengthen Him. Tell about a time when God strengthened you amid adversity.

6. What expectations do we place on God when we pray to Him? Which of our expectations are fair, and which are unfair?

7. The Bible instructs us to "rejoice always, pray without ceasing, give thanks in all circumstances; for this is the will of God in Christ Jesus for you" (1 Thessalonians 5:16–18). What do you understand these words to mean, particularly the command to pray without ceasing?

8. Dedicate a few minutes to fight for others in prayer!

CONCLUSION

Brothers, I do not consider that I have made it my own. But one thing I do: forgetting what lies behind and straining forward to what lies ahead, I press on toward the goal for the prize of the upward call of God in Christ Jesus. Let those of us who are mature think this way, and if in anything you think otherwise, God will reveal that also to you. Only let us hold true to what we have attained.

Philippians 3:13–16

One time, a pastor surveyed his congregation to ask about struggles with forgiveness. He found that many people struggled with forgiving themselves. One man who served in the military killed enemy soldiers in combat. He was haunted by those memories and felt guilty. A woman in her fifties opened up about a decision she'd made in her twenties. She'd been burdened by feelings of regret for the past thirty years. A man had avoided church for years, saying he was so ashamed of his actions that he felt that he just couldn't come back. Keep in mind, all of these people are Christians. One person summed it up well: "I know that God loves me no matter what I've done or been in my life, but to really feel it at the core of my being, I struggle."[15]

Maybe you've wondered, "God forgives me, so why can't I forgive myself?" Each of the examples just cited offers a clue about the obstacle to fully embracing God's forgiveness: our feelings. On the one hand, we know that God removes our sins through Jesus. That belief is the core of our Christian faith. On the other hand, our feelings don't always match

---

15   Adam Hamilton, *Forgiveness: Finding Peace through Letting Go*, 22.

up with our beliefs. Even well-grounded, seasoned Christians can be weighed down by feelings of guilt, shame, disappointment with self, and grief over mistakes. It turns out God is much more gracious to us than we are to ourselves.

The Fiercest Spiritual Battle of All

Perhaps the most difficult spiritual battle we fight is to fully embrace Jesus' gift of forgiveness *for us*. Spiritual warfare rages fiercely when it comes to the sins that burden our consciences. Forgiveness is at the core of God's mission in this world. God values forgiveness so much that He sacrificed His one and only Son to reconcile us to Himself. The devil disrupts our relationship with God by stealing what Jesus died to deliver: the peace of knowing that our sins are forgiven. Satan establishes a stronghold in our hearts when we hold on to our mistakes, shortcomings, and failures. A war rages within each of us to embrace God's forgiveness for *all* of our sins.

I imagine several people in the Bible struggled with the same dilemma that many of us wrestle with: knowing God forgives us but struggling to forgive ourselves. Before his conversion, Paul murdered Christians. He may have struggled with a guilty conscience for a long time. Samson, the Bible's strongman, revealed the secret of his strength and lost it all. What shame he must have felt while tied up and made a public spectacle in the temple of the Philistines. Peter promised Jesus he'd never fall away, and then Peter betrayed his Lord three times. Deeply disappointed in himself, Peter wept bitterly. How Moses must have grieved over his foolish mistake of striking a rock, an act of disobedience that excluded him from the Promised Land.

All of these feelings were wrapped up in one man: King David. Called a man after God's own heart, David let his own heart lead him astray into adultery, deceit, and murder. In Psalm 51:3, he lamented, "For I know my transgressions, and my sin is *ever before me*" (emphasis added). You may know what it feels like to have your sin always before you. All of us mess up. We fall flat on our faces. We drop the ball. We blow it horribly.

But we don't have to define ourselves by our mistakes. Philippians 3 has some key concepts related to self-forgiveness. The first is this: "forgetting what lies behind and straining forward to what lies ahead" (Philippians 3:13). When you're chained down by the past, you can't move forward into the future God has prepared for you. Obsession with your past compromises your future.

A second important concept appears a few verses later: "Only let us hold true to what we have attained" (v. 16). By God's grace, we have already attained the prize. The gift of forgiveness is ours through faith in Jesus. His death on the cross removed our sins from us "as far as the east is from the west" (Psalm 103:12). Our goal is to hold true to what we have attained. Our objective is to fully embrace God's gift of forgiveness.

OVERCOMING
SELF-CONDEMNATION

What gets in the way of embracing God's gift of forgiveness for ourselves? What keeps us from experiencing the full measure of comfort that comes with being forgiven? More often than not, our feelings get in the way. "I know God forgives me, but I don't feel it. I feel guilt, shame, regret, disappointment."

At this point, I'll challenge you with a question: What's in charge, your faith or your feelings? It can't be both. Your faith says Jesus carried your sins on the cross. Your feelings say the burden is still yours to carry. At the end of the day, which message will win? Self-condemnation is a spiritual battle. And in all of our battles, God wants us to know this: victory belongs to the Lord, who declares to each of us, "There is therefore now no condemnation for those who are in Christ Jesus" (Romans 8:1).

As I studied the topic of self-forgiveness, the Holy Spirit directed me to the most wonderful passage tucked away in 1 John 3:18–20: "Little children, let us not love in word or talk but in deed and in truth. By this we shall know that we are of the truth and reassure our heart before Him; for whenever our heart condemns us, God is greater than our heart, and He knows everything."

Our hearts may condemn us. Our feelings may impress the burden of guilt on us. But the Bible proclaims: God is greater than our hearts.

A STRATEGY FOR EMBRACING CHRIST'S FORGIVENESS

We reassure our hearts of God's forgiveness, according to 1 John, by loving in deed and truth. This is the "how" of moving forward from self-condemnation toward the freedom of being a forgiven child of God. If you struggle with the burden of a past action or inaction, read these words carefully: according to the Bible, the best way to reassure your heart of God's grace is to love others in deed and in truth.

This is a very practical teaching. My grandmother used to say, "If you're having a bad day, do something for someone else and you'll feel better." Have you experienced the wisdom of that statement? When we serve someone else, we take the focus off ourselves. Self-condemnation is obsessing about ourselves. Our sins. Our mistakes. Obsessing over ourselves is a prescription for defeat in spiritual warfare.

When we get outside of ourselves, we find liberation. Freedom from self-focus and freedom from guilt go hand in hand.

The best place to redirect our focus? To Jesus. Our faith overcomes our feelings when we focus on Jesus and His mission.

Earlier, I mentioned Peter as an example of guilt and disappointment with self. After His resurrection, Jesus appeared to Peter. For each denial, Jesus now gave Peter an opportunity to confess his love. Three statements of denial. Three statements of love. But there's more. I never noticed this until it was pointed out during a Bible study. After each time Peter reaffirmed his love for Jesus, Jesus gave him a mission: "Feed My lambs. . . . Tend My sheep. . . . Feed My sheep" (John 21:15–17).

Jesus was saying, "Get up, dust yourself off, and serve others." Peter would find healing and new purpose by serving others. The disciple—once stuck in bitter grief—became a bold spokesman, healer, author, evangelist, and ultimately, martyr. The memory of his denial may never have disappeared from his mind completely. But in a very real sense, he did forget what was behind and strain toward what was ahead.

Our faith overcomes our feelings when we focus on Jesus and His mission. We focus on Jesus when we hear and believe His Word. Take Romans 8:1. Write it on an index card, tape it to your mirror, and repeat it out loud every day until it sinks deep into your heart: "There is therefore now no condemnation for those who are in Christ Jesus." Let those words be your battle cry in spiritual warfare!

And then involve yourself in Jesus' mission by serving others. "Feed My lambs. . . . Tend My sheep. . . . Feed My sheep." Sometimes we have to start "doing" and force our feelings to catch up with our actions. You may not feel forgiven right now, but you can act like you're forgiven. You can love others as a forgiven child of God. And by God's grace and in His timing, your feelings *can* conform to your faith. When that happens, God's victory is lived out in your life in powerful ways.

With God's armor, we take hold of the victory that is ours in Jesus. With the belt of truth buckled around our waists, we distinguish what is true from what is a fabrication. The truth is that by faith in Jesus, we are God's saved people, fully forgiven and set free from the prison of our sins. With the breastplate of righteousness covering us, we leave no gaps for Satan's attacks to penetrate to our hearts. Instead, we remember that we are righteous in Christ alone. What we could not do for ourselves, He has done for us.

God's armor helps us to leave the past in the past and to look ahead with hope and joy. With the helmet of salvation atop our heads, God protects our minds so that the pain of the past doesn't overtake us. He reorients our thinking to embrace a more positive, life-giving future. With shoes of peace on our feet, we step forward, not backward, trusting in the firm foundation of Christ. With the shield of faith in place, we ward off the fiery darts of condemnation. With the sword of the Spirit, we counter the devil's distortions of our history with the greater reality that His story reigns supreme in our lives.

DISCUSSION QUESTIONS

1. If someone said to you, "I'm having a hard time forgiving myself," what would you say to comfort that person? How could you apply the content of the chapter to someone who struggles to fully embrace Jesus' gift of forgiveness?

2. Our feelings don't always match up with our beliefs. Why do you think our feelings are so capable of leading us astray from the truth?

3. The chapter states, "Perhaps the most difficult spiritual battle we fight is to fully embrace Jesus' gift of forgiveness *for us*." Do you agree or disagree? Explain your answer.

4. This chapter highlighted several people in the Bible who may have struggled to forgive themselves. Which of them do you think had the hardest time releasing guilt?

5. The Bible speaks of "forgetting what lies behind and straining forward to what lies ahead" (Philippians 3:13). How do these words apply to you? What are you straining forward to right now?

6. Grandmotherly wisdom says, "If you're having a bad day, do something for someone else and you'll feel better." Have you experienced this to be true? Give an example.

7. Generate ideas about specific ways you can love "in deed and in truth" this week.

8. Write three main takeaways you've gained from this book.

STOREHOUSE OF SPIRITUAL WEAPONRY

The following pages contain spiritual weapons loaded with "divine power to destroy strongholds" (2 Corinthians 10:4). When you're fighting spiritual battles, use the following tools to arm yourself with God's gifts. Each section contains these tools:

- Bible verses related to a specific aspect of spiritual warfare. Hebrews 4:12 says, "The Word of God is living and active, sharper than any two-edged sword." Faith holds on to God's Word as the ultimate weapon in the fight for truth.

- A faith affirmation. The faith affirmations are short, Scripture-based sayings you can commit to memory. Whenever you're in a spiritual battle, you can repeat the faith affirmation as a way of reinforcing God's truth in your heart and mind.

- A hymn. Music has a way of touching our emotions and lodging itself in our memories. Sung words often are easier to recall than spoken words. Hymn numbers are from *Lutheran Service Book*.

- A sample prayer. Sometimes we don't know how to pray amid our struggles. These prayers are a starting point for developing your own personalized conversations with God.

Take hold of the weapons God places in your hands and wield them with confidence!

WHEN THE BURDEN OF SIN IS OVERWHELMING, BELIEVE THESE WORDS!

And Peter said to them, "Repent and be baptized every one of you in the name of Jesus Christ for the forgiveness of your sins, and you will receive the gift of the Holy Spirit." (Acts 2:38)

Whoever conceals his transgressions will not prosper, but he who confesses and forsakes them will obtain mercy. (Proverbs 28:13)

And he touched my mouth and said: "Behold, this has touched your lips; your guilt is taken away, and your sin atoned for." (Isaiah 6:7)

If we say we have no sin, we deceive ourselves, and the truth is not in us. If we confess our sins, He is faithful and just to forgive us our sins and to cleanse us from all unrighteousness. (1 John 1:8–9)

He is the propitiation for our sins, and not for ours only but also for the sins of the whole world. (1 John 2:2)

Come now, let us reason together, says the LORD: though your sins are like scarlet, they shall be as white as snow; though they are red like crimson, they shall become like wool. (Isaiah 1:18)

For I will be merciful toward their iniquities, and I will remember their sins no more. (Hebrews 8:12)

For while we were still weak, at the right time Christ died for the ungodly. For one will scarcely die for a righteous person—though perhaps for a good person one would dare even to die—but God shows His love for us in that while we were still sinners, Christ died for us. (Romans 5:6–8)

I, I am He who blots out your transgressions for My own sake, and I will not remember your sins. (Isaiah 43:25)

Who shall bring any charge against God's elect? It is God who justifies. (Romans 8:33)

Blessed is the one whose transgression is forgiven, whose sin is covered. Blessed is the man against whom the LORD counts no iniquity, and in whose spirit there is no deceit. For when I kept silent, my bones wasted away through my groaning all day long. For day and night Your hand was heavy upon me; my strength was dried up as by the heat of summer. I acknowledged my sin to You, and I did not cover my iniquity; I said, "I will confess my transgressions to the LORD," and You forgave the iniquity of my sin. (Psalm 32:1–5)

For our sake He made Him to be sin who knew no sin, so that in Him we might become the righteousness of God. (2 Corinthians 5:21)

FAITH AFFIRMATION:
GOD WILL REMEMBER MY SINS NO MORE.

Chief of sinners though I be,
Jesus shed His blood for me,
Died that I might live on high,
Lives that I might never die.
As the branch is to the vine,
I am His, and He is mine.

Only Jesus can impart
Balm to heal the wounded heart,
Peace that flows from sin forgiv'n,
Joy that lifts the soul to heav'n,
Faith and hope to walk with God
In the way that Enoch trod.

Chief of sinners though I be,
Christ is all in all to me;
All my wants to Him are known,
All my sorrows are His own.
He sustains the hidden life
Safe with Him from earthly strife. (*LSB* 611:1, 3–4)

Lord of mercy, my sins are a burden too heavy for me to carry. Sometimes the guilt feels overwhelming. Please lift my eyes above my sins to behold the cross of Christ. Help me to remember that Jesus took all of my unrighteousness upon Himself by His sacrificial death. Lead me to rejoice that though my sins were as scarlet, they are now as white as snow—completely forgiven and erased. Thank You for giving me a Savior who did for me what I could not do for myself. Because of Jesus, I want to thank and praise You, serve and obey You forever. I pray this in the name of Jesus, who removed my sins as far as the east is from the west. Amen.

When you doubt your salvation, believe these words!

For "everyone who calls on the name of the Lord will be saved." (Romans 10:13)

For I am sure that neither death nor life, nor angels nor rulers, nor things present nor things to come, nor powers, nor height nor depth, nor anything else in all creation, will be able to separate us from the love of God in Christ Jesus our Lord. (Romans 8:38–39)

For God so loved the world, that He gave His only Son, that whoever believes in Him should not perish but have eternal life. (John 3:16)

Since, therefore, we have now been justified by His blood, much more shall we be saved by Him from the wrath of God. (Romans 5:9)

[Jesus said,] "Let not your hearts be troubled. Believe in God; believe also in Me. In My Father's house are many rooms. If it were not so, would I have told you that I go to prepare a place for you? And if I go and prepare a place for you, I will come again and will take you to Myself, that where I am you may be also. And you know the way to where I am going." Thomas said to Him, "Lord, we do not know where You are going. How can we know the way?" Jesus said to him, "I am the way, and the truth, and the life. No one comes to the Father except through Me." (John 14:1–6)

And I am sure of this, that He who began a good work in you will bring it to completion at the day of Jesus Christ. (Philippians 1:6)

For the wages of sin is death, but the free gift of God is eternal life in Christ Jesus our Lord. (Romans 6:23)

[God] saved us and called us to a holy calling, not because of our works but because of His own purpose and grace, which He gave us in Christ Jesus before the ages began. (2 Timothy 1:9)

The saying is trustworthy and deserving of full acceptance, that Christ Jesus came into the world to save sinners, of whom I am the foremost. (1 Timothy 1:15)

FAITH AFFIRMATION:
GOD GAVE HIS ONLY SON TO SAVE ME.

My hope is built on nothing less
Than Jesus' blood and righteousness;
No merit of my own I claim
But wholly lean on Jesus' name.
On Christ, the solid rock, I stand;
All other ground is sinking sand.

When darkness veils His lovely face,
I rest on His unchanging grace;
In ev'ry high and stormy gale
My anchor holds within the veil.
On Christ, the solid rock, I stand;
All other ground is sinking sand.

When He shall come with trumpet sound,
Oh, may I then in Him be found,
Clothed in His righteousness alone,
Redeemed to stand before His throne!
On Christ, the solid rock, I stand;
All other ground is sinking sand. (*LSB* 575:1–2, 4)

Lord of salvation, I'm the foremost of sinners. I admit that I don't deserve a place in Your heavenly kingdom. Right now, I'm plagued by worry that I may not end up in heaven. The thought frightens me beyond description. Through Your Word, impress on my heart the certainty of my salvation in Jesus. Strengthen my faith so that confidence prevails over doubt. You began a good work in me, and Your Word declares that You will complete it. I'm eternally grateful that my salvation is not based on my works but solely on the merits of Christ. I turn my doubts over to You and ask that You would fill me with the joy of Your salvation. I pray this in the name of Jesus, the way, the truth, and the life. Amen.

WHEN YOU'RE STRUGGLING WITH TEMPTATION, BELIEVE THESE WORDS!

No temptation has overtaken you that is not common to man. God is faithful, and He will not let you be tempted beyond your ability, but with the temptation He will also provide the way of escape, that you may be able to endure it. (1 Corinthians 10:13)

Do not be conformed to this world, but be transformed by the renewal of your mind, that by testing you may discern what is the will of God, what is good and acceptable and perfect. (Romans 12:2)

Count it all joy, my brothers, when you meet trials of various kinds, for you know that the testing of your faith produces steadfastness. (James 1:2–3)

[Jesus said,] "Watch and pray that you may not enter into temptation. The spirit indeed is willing, but the flesh is weak." (Matthew 26:41)

For we do not have a high priest who is unable to sympathize with our weaknesses, but one who in every

respect has been tempted as we are, yet without sin.
(Hebrews 4:15)

The Lord knows how to rescue the godly from trials.
(2 Peter 2:9)

Since therefore the children share in flesh and blood,
He Himself likewise partook of the same things, that
through death He might destroy the one who has the
power of death, that is, the devil, and deliver all those
who through fear of death were subject to lifelong
slavery. For surely it is not angels that He helps, but
He helps the offspring of Abraham. Therefore He had
to be made like His brothers in every respect, so that
He might become a merciful and faithful high priest
in the service of God, to make propitiation for the sins
of the people. For because He Himself has suffered
when tempted, He is able to help those who are being
tempted. (Hebrews 2:14–18)

I have been crucified with Christ. It is no longer I who live,
but Christ who lives in me. And the life I now live in the
flesh I live by faith in the Son of God, who loved me and
gave Himself for me. (Galatians 2:20)

FAITH AFFIRMATION:
I CAN RESIST BECAUSE CHRIST LIVES IN ME.

Rise, my soul, to watch and pray;
From your sleep awaken!
Be not by the evil day
Unawares o'ertaken;
For the foe,
Well we know,
Is a harvest reaping
While the saints are sleeping.

Watch against the devil's snares
Lest asleep he find you;
For indeed no pains he spares
To deceive and blind you.
Satan's prey
Oft are they
Who secure are sleeping
And no watch are keeping.

Watch! Let not the wicked world
With its lies defeat you
Lest with bold deceptions hurled
It betray and cheat you.
Watch and see
Lest there be
Faithless friends to charm you,
Who but seek to harm you.

Watch against yourself, my soul,
Lest with grace you trifle;
Let not self your thoughts control
Nor God's mercy stifle.
Pride and sin
Lurk within,
All your hopes to shatter;
Heed not when they flatter.

But while watching, also pray
To the Lord unceasing.
God protects you day by day,
Strength and faith increasing,
So that still
Mind and will
Shall unite to serve Him
And forever love Him. (*LSB* 663)

Faithful Lord, my spirit is willing, but my flesh is weak. The enemy knows my vulnerabilities far too well. Temptation is knocking at my door, and I'm inclined to open it. I want to do what is right, but I fear that sin is going to get the best of me—again. Strengthen me against temptation. By Your grace, I can hold out. By Your power, I can overcome. I count on You to provide a way out so that I may endure this time of testing without falling into sin. Toughen my resolve. Fortify my defenses. Bring me to the other side of this trial with a stronger faith and greater ability to withstand future temptations. I pray this in the name of Jesus, who resisted temptation flawlessly and died for me as the spotless Lamb of God. Amen.

WHEN YOU FEEL OUTMATCHED BY THE ENEMY, BELIEVE THESE WORDS!

Since therefore the children share in flesh and blood, He Himself likewise partook of the same things, that through death He might destroy the one who has the power of death, that is, the devil. (Hebrews 2:14)

Be sober-minded; be watchful. Your adversary the devil prowls around like a roaring lion, seeking someone to devour. Resist him, firm in your faith, knowing that the same kinds of suffering are being experienced by your brotherhood throughout the world. (1 Peter 5:8–9)

But the Lord is faithful. He will establish you and guard you against the evil one. (2 Thessalonians 3:3)

And the devil who had deceived them was thrown into the lake of fire and sulfur where the beast and the false prophet were, and they will be tormented day and night forever and ever. (Revelation 20:10)

And I heard a loud voice in heaven, saying, "Now the salvation and the power and the kingdom of our God and the authority of His Christ have come, for the accuser of our brothers has been thrown down, who accuses them day and night before our God. And they have conquered him by the blood of the Lamb and by the word of their testimony, for they loved not their lives even unto death. Therefore, rejoice, O heavens and you who dwell in them! But woe to you, O earth and sea, for the devil has come down to you in great wrath, because he knows that his time is short!" (Revelation 12:10–12)

Now is the judgment of this world; now will the ruler of this world be cast out. (John 12:31)

Little children, you are from God and have overcome them, for He who is in you is greater than he who is in the world. (1 John 4:4)

Submit yourselves therefore to God. Resist the devil, and he will flee from you. (James 4:7)

FAITH AFFIRMATION:
GOD WILL GUARD ME AGAINST THE EVIL ONE.

A mighty fortress is our God,
A trusty shield and weapon;
He helps us free from ev'ry need
That hath us now o'ertaken.
The old evil foe
Now means deadly woe;
Deep guile and great might
Are his dread arms in fight;
On earth is not his equal.

Though devils all the world should fill,
All eager to devour us,

We tremble not, we fear no ill;
They shall not overpow'r us.
This world's prince may still
Scowl fierce as he will,
He can harm us none.
He's judged; the deed is done;
One little word can fell him. (*LSB* 656:1, 3)

Victorious Lord, the enemy is doing his worst against me. He's a formidable foe. At times, I feel that he's outmaneuvering me at every turn. Lord Jesus, You have already defeated Satan. Please apply Your power in full force in my current battle with the evil one. You crushed him on the cross. Disarm him now so that he may have no power over me. Help me to identify his schemes, resist his tactics, and spoil his plans for my downfall. I belong to You. Satan has no claim on me. I pray this in Your name, Jesus, my conquering King. Amen.

WHEN YOU'RE SPIRITUALLY EXHAUSTED, BELIEVE THESE WORDS!

Have you not known? Have you not heard? The LORD is the
everlasting God, the Creator of the ends of the earth.
He does not faint or grow weary; His understanding is
unsearchable. He gives power to the faint, and to him
who has no might He increases strength. Even youths
shall faint and be weary, and young men shall fall
exhausted; but they who wait for the LORD shall renew
their strength; they shall mount up with wings like
eagles; they shall run and not be weary; they shall walk
and not faint. (Isaiah 40:28–31)

My flesh and my heart may fail, but God is the strength of
my heart and my portion forever. (Psalm 73:26)

But He said to me, "My grace is sufficient for you, for My power is made perfect in weakness." Therefore I will boast all the more gladly of my weaknesses, so that the power of Christ may rest upon me. For the sake of Christ, then, I am content with weaknesses, insults, hardships, persecutions, and calamities. For when I am weak, then I am strong. (2 Corinthians 12:9–10)

GOD, the Lord, is my strength; He makes my feet like the deer's; He makes me tread on my high places. (Habakkuk 3:19)

Therefore, since we are surrounded by so great a cloud of witnesses, let us also lay aside every weight, and sin which clings so closely, and let us run with endurance the race that is set before us, looking to Jesus, the founder and perfecter of our faith, who for the joy that was set before Him endured the cross, despising the shame, and is seated at the right hand of the throne of God. Consider Him who endured from sinners such hostility against Himself, so that you may not grow weary or fainthearted. (Hebrews 12:1–3)

You then, my child, be strengthened by the grace that is in Christ Jesus. (2 Timothy 2:1)

We are afflicted in every way, but not crushed; perplexed, but not driven to despair; persecuted, but not forsaken; struck down, but not destroyed; always carrying in the body the death of Jesus, so that the life of Jesus may also be manifested in our bodies. For we who live are always being given over to death for Jesus' sake, so that the life of Jesus also may be manifested in our mortal flesh. (2 Corinthians 4:8–11)

Fear not, for I am with you; be not dismayed, for I am
your God; I will strengthen you, I will help you, I will
uphold you with My righteous right hand. (Isaiah 41:10)

FAITH AFFIRMATION:
GOD'S POWER IS MADE PERFECT IN MY WEAKNESS.

How firm a foundation, O saints of the Lord,
Is laid for your faith in His excellent Word!
What more can He say than to you He has said
Who unto the Savior for refuge have fled?

"Fear not! I am with you, O be not dismayed,
For I am your God and will still give you aid;
I'll strengthen you, help you, and cause you to stand,
Upheld by My righteous, omnipotent hand." (*LSB* 728:1–2)

Lord of renewal and strength, I'm tired. My energy is depleted.
Everything I've been through lately has taken its toll, and I'm spent. In
my weakness, please be my strength. My inner resources may run out,
but Yours never do. Restore my energy so that I may mount up with
wings like eagles, may run and not be weary, may walk and not faint.
The only way forward is with You. I pray this in the name of Jesus,
whose grace is more than sufficient for me. Amen.

WHEN YOU NEED SPIRITUAL PROTECTION, BELIEVE THESE WORDS!

He who dwells in the shelter of the Most High will abide
in the shadow of the Almighty. I will say to the LORD,
"My refuge and my fortress, my God, in whom I trust."
For He will deliver you from the snare of the fowler
and from the deadly pestilence. He will cover you with

His pinions, and under His wings you will find refuge. (Psalm 91:1–4)

Because you have made the LORD your dwelling place—the Most High, who is my refuge—no evil shall be allowed to befall you, no plague come near your tent. For He will command His angels concerning you to guard you in all your ways. (Psalm 91:9–11)

The LORD will cause your enemies who rise against you to be defeated before you. They shall come out against you one way and flee before you seven ways. (Deuteronomy 28:7)

I love You, O LORD, my strength. The LORD is my rock and my fortress and my deliverer, my God, my rock, in whom I take refuge, my shield, and the horn of my salvation, my stronghold. (Psalm 18:1–2)

But I will sing of Your strength; I will sing aloud of Your steadfast love in the morning. For You have been to me a fortress and a refuge in the day of my distress. (Psalm 59:16)

When the servant of the man of God rose early in the morning and went out, behold, an army with horses and chariots was all around the city. And the servant said, "Alas, my master! What shall we do?" He said, "Do not be afraid, for those who are with us are more than those who are with them." Then Elisha prayed and said, "O LORD, please open his eyes that he may see." So the LORD opened the eyes of the young man, and he saw, and behold, the mountain was full of horses and chariots of fire all around Elisha. (2 Kings 6:15–17)

When you pass through the waters, I will be with you; and through the rivers, they shall not overwhelm you;

when you walk through fire you shall not be burned,
and the flame shall not consume you. (Isaiah 43:2)

God is our refuge and strength, a very present help in
trouble. (Psalm 46:1)

FAITH AFFIRMATION:
GOD IS MY REFUGE AND STRENGTH.

Have no fear, little flock;
Have no fear, little flock,
For the Father has chosen
To give you the Kingdom;
Have no fear, little flock!

Have good cheer, little flock;
Have good cheer, little flock,
For the Father will keep you
In His love forever;
Have good cheer, little flock! (*LSB* 735:1–2)

Lord God, my dwelling place and refuge, trouble is all around. Dangers encircle me. Illness. Natural disasters. Criminal activity. Terrorism. And these are just the physical threats. My spirit is under attack constantly. I need Your protection in every way. When I'm afraid of danger, remind me that Your heavenly army is well equipped and ready to fight. Send Your holy angels to protect me from all evil. Guard me with Your love. I pray this in the name of Jesus, who walked on the water and passed through the fires of suffering for my sake. Amen.

WHEN YOU'RE ASSAULTED BY LIES, BELIEVE THESE WORDS!

Finally, brothers, whatever is true, whatever is honorable, whatever is just, whatever is pure, whatever is lovely, whatever is commendable, if there is any excellence, if there is anything worthy of praise, think about these things. (Philippians 4:8)

[Jesus said to His opponents,] "You are of your father the devil, and your will is to do your father's desires. He was a murderer from the beginning, and does not stand in the truth, because there is no truth in him. When he lies, he speaks out of his own character, for he is a liar and the father of lies." (John 8:44)

Beloved, do not believe every spirit, but test the spirits to see whether they are from God, for many false prophets have gone out into the world. (1 John 4:1)

When the Spirit of truth comes, He will guide you into all the truth, for He will not speak on His own authority, but whatever He hears He will speak, and He will declare to you the things that are to come. (John 16:13)

See to it that no one takes you captive by philosophy and empty deceit, according to human tradition, according to the elemental spirits of the world, and not according to Christ. (Colossians 2:8)

Sanctify them in the truth; Your word is truth. (John 17:17)

And you will know the truth, and the truth will set you free. (John 8:32)

FAITH AFFIRMATION:
THE SPIRIT WILL LEAD ME INTO ALL TRUTH.

I heard the voice of Jesus say,
"Come unto Me and rest;
Lay down, thou weary one, lay down
Thy head upon My breast."
I came to Jesus as I was,
So weary, worn, and sad;
I found in Him a resting place,
And He has made me glad.

I heard the voice of Jesus say,
"I am this dark world's light.
Look unto Me; thy morn shall rise
And all thy day be bright."
I looked to Jesus, and I found
In Him my star, my sun;
And in that light of life I'll walk
Till trav'ling days are done. (*LSB* 699:1, 3)

Lord of truth, sometimes it's hard to separate fact from falsehood. The enemy has a way of getting in my head. He impresses lies upon me. He's cunning and persuasive. Too often, I lose sight of what is true and believe a distortion of reality. I believe lies about You, about others, and about myself. As a result, my trust in You falters, my love for others fails, and my self-worth plummets. Rescue me from lies. Banish them. By Your Spirit of truth, guide me into all truth. Give me a discerning spirit so that I will not be taken captive by empty deceit. Set my feet firmly on the solid ground of Your Word and keep me there. I pray this in the name of Jesus, the Truth who has set me free. Amen.

WHEN YOU'RE STRUGGLING WITH BITTERNESS OR RESENTMENT, BELIEVE THESE WORDS!

Let all bitterness and wrath and anger and clamor and slander be put away from you, along with all malice. Be kind to one another, tenderhearted, forgiving one another, as God in Christ forgave you. (Ephesians 4:31–32)

Put on then, as God's chosen ones, holy and beloved, compassionate hearts, kindness, humility, meekness, and patience, bearing with one another and, if one has a complaint against another, forgiving each other; as the Lord has forgiven you, so you also must forgive. And above all these put on love, which binds everything together in perfect harmony. (Colossians 3:12–14)

See to it that no one fails to obtain the grace of God; that no "root of bitterness" springs up and causes trouble, and by it many become defiled. (Hebrews 12:15)

And whenever you stand praying, forgive, if you have anything against anyone, so that your Father also who is in heaven may forgive you your trespasses. (Mark 11:25)

Hatred stirs up strife, but love covers all offenses. (Proverbs 10:12)

Be not quick in your spirit to become angry, for anger lodges in the heart of fools. (Ecclesiastes 7:9)

Repay no one evil for evil, but give thought to do what is honorable in the sight of all. If possible, so far as it depends on you, live peaceably with all. . . . Do not be overcome by evil, but overcome evil with good. (Romans 12:17–18, 21)

> Good sense makes one slow to anger, and it is his glory to overlook an offense. (Proverbs 19:11)

> Be angry and do not sin; do not let the sun go down on your anger. (Ephesians 4:26)

FAITH AFFIRMATION:
FORGIVE—AS THE LORD HAS FORGIVEN ME.

Lord of all nations, grant me grace
To love all people, ev'ry race;
And in each person may I see
My kindred, loved, redeemed by Thee.

Break down the wall that would divide
Thy children, Lord, on ev'ry side.
My neighbor's good let me pursue;
Let Christian love bind warm and true.

With Thine own love may I be filled
And by Thy Holy Spirit willed,
That all I touch, where'er I be,
May be divinely touched by Thee. (*LSB* 844:1–2, 5)

Gracious Lord, who overlooks my offenses for the sake of Christ, I find myself stuck in bitterness. I've been hurt, and the pain still stings. Lord, I don't want resentment to define me. I don't want the pain to drag me down any longer. Please give me a full measure of Your grace so that the root of bitterness is cut off and withers. Give me grace to forgive others as You in Christ have so graciously forgiven me. Help me to move beyond the pain of the past to the possibilities of a new and better future. Cultivate within me a compassionate heart, kindness, humility, meekness, patience, and love. I pray this in the name of Jesus, who on the cross overcame evil with the ultimate good. Amen.

WHEN YOUR PAST IS TORMENTING YOU, BELIEVE THESE WORDS!

We know that our old self was crucified with Him in order that the body of sin might be brought to nothing, so that we would no longer be enslaved to sin. For one who has died has been set free from sin. (Romans 6:6–7)

Let us draw near with a true heart in full assurance of faith, with our hearts sprinkled clean from an evil conscience and our bodies washed with pure water. (Hebrews 10:22)

There is therefore now no condemnation for those who are in Christ Jesus. For the law of the Spirit of life has set you free in Christ Jesus from the law of sin and death. (Romans 8:1–2)

Therefore, if anyone is in Christ, he is a new creation. The old has passed away; behold, the new has come. (2 Corinthians 5:17)

The LORD is merciful and gracious, slow to anger and abounding in steadfast love. He will not always chide, nor will He keep His anger forever. He does not deal with us according to our sins, nor repay us according to our iniquities. For as high as the heavens are above the earth, so great is His steadfast love toward those who fear Him; as far as the east is from the west, so far does He remove our transgressions from us. (Psalm 103:8–12)

My little children, I am writing these things to you so that you may not sin. But if anyone does sin, we have an

advocate with the Father, Jesus Christ the righteous.
(1 John 2:1)

For godly grief produces a repentance that leads to salvation without regret, whereas worldly grief produces
death. (2 Corinthians 7:10)

FAITH AFFIRMATION:
IN CHRIST, I AM A NEW CREATION.

Love divine, all loves excelling,
Joy of heav'n, to earth come down!
Fix in us Thy humble dwelling,
All Thy faithful mercies crown.
Jesus, Thou art all compassion,
Pure, unbounded love Thou art;
Visit us with Thy salvation,
Enter ev'ry trembling heart.

Breathe, O breathe Thy loving Spirit
Into ev'ry troubled breast;
Let us all in Thee inherit;
Let us find Thy promised rest.
Take away the love of sinning;
Alpha and Omega be;
End of faith, as its beginning,
Set our hearts at liberty.

Finish then Thy new creation,
Pure and spotless let us be;
Let us see Thy great salvation
Perfectly restored in Thee,
Changed from glory into glory,
Till in heav'n we take our place,
Till we cast our crowns before Thee,
Lost in wonder, love, and praise! (*LSB* 700:1–2, 4)

Lord of new beginnings, if only life offered second chances. You know there are things I'd do differently. Right now, I'm stuck, obsessing over my sins and dwelling on my missteps. The very mistakes I was determined never to do, I did. I grieve those actions deeply. Lord, refashion my feelings into a godly grief, the kind that produces repentance and leads to salvation without regret. Because You do not condemn me, rescue me from self-condemnation. Cleanse my conscience as You have cleansed my soul with the blood of Christ. Point me forward in hope and lead me on a joyful path. I pray this in the name of Jesus, who has freed me from the curse of sin and made me a new creation. Amen.

WHEN GOD SEEMS DISTANT, BELIEVE THESE WORDS!

Draw near to God, and He will draw near to you. (James 4:8a)

Let us then with confidence draw near to the throne of grace, that we may receive mercy and find grace to help in time of need. (Hebrews 4:16)

The LORD is near to all who call on Him, to all who call on Him in truth. (Psalm 145:18)

Can a man hide himself in secret places so that I cannot see him? declares the LORD. Do I not fill heaven and earth? declares the LORD. (Jeremiah 23:24)

Or do you not know that your body is a temple of the Holy Spirit within you, whom you have from God? You are not your own. (1 Corinthians 6:19)

Behold, I am with you always, to the end of the age. (Matthew 28:20b)

Be strong and courageous. Do not fear or be in dread of them, for it is the LORD your God who goes with you. He will not leave you or forsake you. (Deuteronomy 31:6)

> Where shall I go from Your Spirit? Or where shall I flee
> from Your presence? If I ascend to heaven, You are
> there! If I make my bed in Sheol, You are there! If I take
> the wings of the morning and dwell in the uttermost
> parts of the sea, even there Your hand shall lead me,
> and Your right hand shall hold me. (Psalm 139:7–10)

FAITH AFFIRMATION:
JESUS IS WITH ME ALWAYS.

I know that my Redeemer lives;
What comfort this sweet sentence gives!
He lives, He lives, who once was dead;
He lives, my ever-living head.

He lives to bless me with His love;
He lives to plead for me above;
He lives my hungry soul to feed;
He lives to help in time of need.

He lives to grant me rich supply;
He lives to guide me with His eye;
He lives to comfort me when faint;
He lives to hear my soul's complaint.

He lives to silence all my fears;
He lives to wipe away my tears;
He lives to calm my troubled heart;
He lives all blessings to impart.

He lives, all glory to His name!
He lives, my Jesus, still the same;
Oh, the sweet joy this sentence gives:
I know that my Redeemer lives! (LSB 461:1, 3–5, 8)

Lord, are You there? I know You are. You fill heaven and earth. I know
that intellectually, but sometimes my heart forgets. When problems are

unceasing, sometimes it feels like You've turned Your attention away from me. I need my faith to prevail over my feelings. I know You're near. Where shall I go from Your Spirit? Nowhere! Where shall I flee from Your presence? There's not a single place! Comfort me with the truth that You are with me in all things. You are my very present help in times of trouble. You have promised to be with me always. Therefore, I call upon You in the name of Jesus, who is with me always, to the end of the age. Amen.

WHEN YOU FEEL ANXIOUS OR WORRIED, BELIEVE THESE WORDS!

For God gave us a spirit not of fear but of power and love and self-control. (2 Timothy 1:7)

Do not be anxious about anything, but in everything by prayer and supplication with thanksgiving let your requests be made known to God. And the peace of God, which surpasses all understanding, will guard your hearts and your minds in Christ Jesus. (Philippians 4:6–7)

Have I not commanded you? Be strong and coura-geous. Do not be frightened, and do not be dismayed, for the LORD your God is with you wherever you go. (Joshua 1:9)

And He said to His disciples, "Therefore I tell you, do not be anxious about your life, what you will eat, nor about your body, what you will put on." (Luke 12:22)

When the cares of my heart are many, Your consolations cheer my soul. (Psalm 94:19)

Blessed is the man who trusts in the LORD, whose trust is the LORD. He is like a tree planted by water, that sends out its roots by the stream, and does not fear when heat comes, for its leaves remain green, and is not anxious in the year of drought, for it does not cease to bear fruit. (Jeremiah 17:7–8)

When I am afraid, I put my trust in You. (Psalm 56:3)

[Jesus said,] "Come to Me, all who labor and are heavy laden, and I will give you rest. Take My yoke upon you, and learn from Me, for I am gentle and lowly in heart, and you will find rest for your souls. For My yoke is easy, and My burden is light." (Matthew 11:28–30)

I sought the LORD, and He answered me and delivered me from all my fears. (Psalm 34:4)

Cast your burden on the LORD, and He will sustain you; He will never permit the righteous to be moved. (Psalm 55:22)

FAITH AFFIRMATION:
WHEN I AM AFRAID, I PUT MY TRUST IN GOD.

Be still, my soul; the Lord is on your side;
Bear patiently the cross of grief or pain;
Leave to your God to order and provide;
In ev'ry change He faithful will remain.
Be still, my soul; your best, your heav'nly Friend
Through thorny ways leads to a joyful end.

Be still, my soul; your God will undertake
To guide the future as He has the past.
Your hope, your confidence let nothing shake;
All now mysterious shall be bright at last.
Be still, my soul; the waves and winds still know
His voice who ruled them while He dwelt below.
(*LSB* 752:1–2)

Faithful Lord, I'm anxious. The concerns of life are dominating my thoughts. Please rescue me from worry. Cast out the spirit of fear that has taken hold of me. Soothe my anxious heart. Cheer my soul. Stir up the true spirit You have given me, a spirit of power and love and self-control. Give me courage in the face of all my fears. I need You to carry my burden. It's too much for me but never too much for You. Now, in this prayer, I lay my anxieties at the foot of the cross. I pray this in the name of Jesus, who lightens my burden and gives rest to my soul. Amen.

WHEN INNER CONFLICT IS REIGNING, BELIEVE THESE WORDS!

[Jesus said,] "Peace I leave with you; My peace I give to you. Not as the world gives do I give to you. Let not your hearts be troubled, neither let them be afraid." (John 14:27)

Now may the Lord of peace Himself give you peace at all times in every way. The Lord be with you all. (2 Thessalonians 3:16)

Therefore, since we have been justified by faith, we have peace with God through our Lord Jesus Christ. (Romans 5:1)

The LORD is my shepherd; I shall not want. He makes me lie down in green pastures. He leads me beside still waters. He restores my soul. He leads me in paths of righteousness for His name's sake. Even though I walk through the valley of the shadow of death, I will fear no evil, for You are with me; Your rod and Your staff, they comfort me. You prepare a table before me in the presence of my enemies; You anoint my head with oil; my cup overflows. Surely goodness and mercy shall follow me all the days of my life, and I shall dwell in the house of the LORD forever. (Psalm 23)

And let the peace of Christ rule in your hearts, to which indeed you were called in one body. And be thankful. (Colossians 3:15)

May the LORD give strength to His people! May the LORD bless His people with peace! (Psalm 29:11)

I have said these things to you, that in Me you may have peace. In the world you will have tribulation. But take heart; I have overcome the world. (John 16:33)

May the God of hope fill you with all joy and peace in believing, so that by the power of the Holy Spirit you may abound in hope. (Romans 15:13)

You keep him in perfect peace whose mind is stayed on You, because he trusts in You. (Isaiah 26:3)

FAITH AFFIRMATION:
THE PEACE OF CHRIST RULES IN MY HEART.

Rock of Ages, cleft for me,
Let me hide myself in Thee;
Let the water and the blood,
From Thy riven side which flowed,
Be of sin the double cure:
Cleanse me from its guilt and pow'r.

Nothing in my hand I bring;
Simply to Thy cross I cling.
Naked, come to Thee for dress;
Helpless, look to Thee for grace;
Foul, I to the fountain fly;
Wash me, Savior, or I die. (*LSB* 761:1, 3)

Lord of peace, a war rages within me. I'm terribly unsettled. On the outside, I may look fine. But on the inside, I'm deeply conflicted. My conscience is restless. The tribulations of life have left me broken, torn, and disoriented. I've tried to conjure up peace inside of myself, but that doesn't work. I've looked for satisfaction in other places, and it's fleeting. You are the only source of true and lasting peace, and that's what I so deeply desire. Help me to dwell on Your promises. I'm ready for the peace of Christ to rule in my heart. Please grant me Your peace in full measure today. I pray this in the name of Jesus, who has overcome the world and can overcome all that troubles me. Amen.

WHEN YOU'RE STRUGGLING TO MOVE FORWARD, BELIEVE THESE WORDS!

Brothers, I do not consider that I have made it my own. But one thing I do: forgetting what lies behind and straining forward to what lies ahead, I press on toward the goal for the prize of the upward call of God in Christ Jesus. (Philippians 3:13–14)

Repent therefore, and turn back, that your sins may be blotted out, that times of refreshing may come from the presence of the Lord. (Acts 3:19–20)

The LORD will fulfill His purpose for me; Your steadfast love, O LORD, endures forever. Do not forsake the work of Your hands. (Psalm 138:8)

For everyone who has been born of God overcomes the world. And this is the victory that has overcome the world—our faith. Who is it that overcomes the world except the one who believes that Jesus is the Son of God? (1 John 5:4–5)

No, in all these things we are more than conquerors through Him who loved us. (Romans 8:37)

Now to Him who is able to do far more abundantly than all that we ask or think, according to the power at work within us, to Him be glory in the church and in Christ Jesus throughout all generations, forever and ever. Amen. (Ephesians 3:20–21)

But thanks be to God, who gives us the victory through our Lord Jesus Christ. (1 Corinthians 15:57)

FAITH AFFIRMATION:
IN CHRIST, I PRESS ON TOWARD THE GOAL.

Guide me, O Thou great Redeemer,
Pilgrim through this barren land.
I am weak, but Thou art mighty;
Hold me with Thy pow'rful hand.
Bread of heaven, bread of heaven,
Feed me till I want no more;
Feed me till I want no more.

Open now the crystal fountain
Whence the healing stream doth flow;
Let the fiery, cloudy pillar
Lead me all my journey through.
Strong deliv'rer, strong deliv'rer,
Be Thou still my strength and shield;
Be Thou still my strength and shield.

When I tread the verge of Jordan,
Bid my anxious fears subside;
Death of death and hell's destruction,
Land me safe on Canaan's side.
Songs of praises, songs of praises
I will ever give to Thee;
I will ever give to Thee. (*LSB* 918)

Lord of the upward call, You have cast my sights forward. The enemy wants to drag me into the past and fill my heart with regret and despair. You have given me a better and higher calling. Make me forgetful—forgetting what lies behind and straining forward to what lies ahead. I'm ready to move ahead to what You have planned for me. I am freed from the chains of yesterday; lead me into tomorrow with a joyful and hopeful spirit. Your victory is my victory in Christ. I stand in that victory right now, facing forward and upward. To You be all glory, honor, and praise! I pray this in the name of Jesus, the conquering Lord. Amen.

LEADER GUIDE

The saying is true—there is strength in numbers. It's not just a matter of practical insight but also a biblical truth: "Two are better than one, because they have a good reward for their toil. For if they fall, one will lift up his fellow. But woe to him who is alone when he falls and has not another to lift him up!" (Ecclesiastes 4:9–10).

This book is a tool for individuals to support one another in spiritual warfare. One can fight the battle alone. Two fighting together are stronger. No one needs to fight the devil alone or battle evil solo. God places others in our lives who can come alongside us in spiritual warfare.

Our strength comes from the Savior, who stands beside us in the battle. Jesus promises, "For where two or three are gathered in My name, there am I among them" (Matthew 18:20). Jesus is always present in our lives, every moment of every day. Yet in these words, He promises to be present in an extra special way when two or more come together in His name.

As a group, consider yourselves to be an army under the leadership of Jesus, fighting against the darkness. You're tightening the armor of God around one another, securing it more firmly in place. You're coming alongside one another in battle, linking your shields as soldiers of the cross.

The following pages are a guide to assist leaders in facilitating group discussion, but they may also be helpful to individual readers looking for guidance about the discussion questions. If you're leading a group study, encourage participants to write down their answers before you meet as a group so that everyone has thoughtfully prepared for the discussion time. During group discussion, take your time. It's better to dwell on a question that generates good conversation than to rush through the material. You might prioritize questions ahead of time in case you need to skip some.

When you finish the study, remember to celebrate! Ask group members what they want to study next. Although this study is finished, our care and encouragement for one another never end. Take time to check in with one another and pray without ceasing for one another!

God bless you as you take hold of the truth expressed in His Word!

UNMASKING THE ENEMY
Introduction

1. When you hear the phrase "spiritual warfare," what comes to mind?

    This question offers a good opportunity to identify preconceived ideas about spiritual warfare. Some may think of it as merely a mental game. Others may have more extreme ideas of demonic possession, exorcisms, and the like. Listen to everyone's answers with equal respect and consideration. After hearing everyone's responses, direct the group back to the definition in the chapter: "Spiritual warfare is the battle over your spirit." Remind them that it's more than just having a bad day. We're in the midst of a true battle every day!

2. How do you feel, knowing that there is a battle raging, and you are the prize?

    Be prepared for a variety of answers. For some, the idea may feel threatening and frightful. For others, the idea of being a prize may be totally foreign. Reinforce that each person is a valuable prize because of the value *God* has assigned to them.

3. How did the chapter confirm, challenge, or reshape your views of the devil?

    The question can be divided into two parts. The first part is to reflect on the devil's origins. Do group members know that he originally was an exalted angel who was cast down from heaven? The second part is to reflect on the devil's tactics. His chief tactic is deception. You might

probe to see if group members assign more power to the devil than Scripture says he really has.

4. Jesus said, "I saw Satan fall like lightning from heaven" (Luke 10:18). The devil's pride was his downfall. In which area of your life are you most tempted toward pride?

A definition of *pride* is "pleasure or satisfaction in one's accomplishments or possessions." You might ask participants to think of their own accomplishments or possessions and how the devil might tempt them toward sinful self-absorption. Respect the rights of participants to pass if they feel uncomfortable being vulnerable with the group in this first session. Over future sessions, they may become more willing to open up.

5. Jesus called the devil "the father of lies" (John 8:44). Where do you feel the devil is most active in spreading lies right now?

You might read John 8:39–47 for the context behind Jesus' words. The question can be considered on various levels. What lies do we believe in our families? in our workplaces? in our own minds? What lies are being proliferated in our society? (Take care not to get sidetracked by any soapboxes or political discussions.)

6. Name a struggle in your life. Think of how the devil might try to assign a distorted meaning to your struggle. Now reframe your struggle and describe it from a perspective of faith in God's goodness and purpose.

This question invites personal reflection. Allow group members to give a detailed answer or a vague response, whichever is more comfortable for them at this point in the study. You might allow one person to be the case study for the group. For example, a mom might share her struggles in parenting young children. The devil might influence her to think she's unqualified as a mom, incompetent, or a failure. Reframing the issue, the group can help her to see reality from God's eyes. God has made her the mother to her children for a purpose. He has gifted her and is helping her to grow daily as a parent.

7. What is the difference between Jesus' role and our role in spiritual warfare? What does it look like for us to resist?

Review what the chapter says about Jesus' role and ours. Place the focus on Jesus' work of defeating the devil on the cross. Only Jesus is powerful enough to defeat the devil. We resist with the gifts God gives us. Those gifts are described as the armor of God. Use this question to build excitement about what is to come in the study. In the chapters ahead, you'll learn about the tools of resistance that God graciously provides.

8. Write down goals that you hope to achieve by reading this book. What about spiritual warfare do you want to understand better?

Encourage participants to list one or more goals. Goals might be based on a current struggle, such as believing lies or having doubts about their faith. A goal could be something they hope to learn about spiritual warfare. A goal also could be an action they hope to take out of a greater sense of confidence and direction. Strive for specificity as much as possible.

CHAPTER 1

1. Have your emotions ever clouded your ability to recognize truth? Explain.

   An example might be a time when you were defensive and couldn't see the valid point someone was trying to make. Or maybe you've held an opinion for a long time and struggled to be open-minded to new possibilities. As the leader, go first by giving an example from your life, opening the door for others to share.

2. What do you think Jesus meant when He said, "The truth will set you free" (John 8:32)? How does truth liberate?

   You might consider the opposite as well: how do lies imprison us? Lies keep us trapped in a false reality. Truth liberates by keeping us in reality, which is often not as bad as the scenarios we fear. Encourage group members to think of examples of truth setting someone free.

3. Why do you suppose the Bible warns against self-deceit more than the devil's deceitfulness?

   We can be our own worst enemy. From a biblical perspective, it's not an acceptable excuse to say, "The devil made me do it." Our sinful nature blinds us to truth. Romans 7:7–25 could be helpful reading on our constant internal struggle with sin.

4. What do you think is the most prevalent type of self-deception?

Two examples were provided in the chapter: "A little more won't hurt" and "One more time won't do any harm. No one will know." The first self-deception tests the boundaries of excess. The second is the temptation to operate in the darkness. Participants don't need to name specific sins of self-deception. General categories will work. For example, sometimes we deceive ourselves by excusing harshness under the label of righteous anger.

5.   "Along with His resurrection on the third day, Jesus' work on the cross is the greatest truth of all." How would you explain the significance of this statement to someone who knows very little about Christ?

Envision the perspective of an unbeliever or new Christian. Discuss the importance of the cross and empty tomb as the central teachings of the Christian faith. Direct participants to 1 Corinthians 15:17, which says that if Christ has not been raised, our faith is in vain. Discuss how other truths of the Christian faith connect back to Jesus' atoning work for us.

6.   Read Philippians 4:8. The verse tells us what kinds of things to think about. Choose two or three words from the list and give concrete examples to match those words.

This is a great opportunity to celebrate what is good in our world. Discuss how God abiding in us enables us to focus on the positive, even amid dire circumstances.

7   What worries you? What does God want you to do with your worry?

Write down the group's responses. These answers can be excellent material for prayer requests or follow-up during the week. God invites us to bring our worries to Him. See 1 Peter 5:7. As the chapter states, God wants us to fix our minds on what is good instead of fixing our minds on what worries us.

8. Name three truths about who you are in God's eyes.

This question is designed for personal affirmation according to God's Word and truth. Some possible answers are "a child of God," "forgiven," and "set free." Encourage participants to elaborate on their answers. Affirm all answers that reinforce God's love. If anyone says something negative, such as "I'm a disappointment," emphasize God's grace and follow up with a one-on-one conversation after the study.

CHAPTER 2

1. What do you know about Martin Luther? How does it feel to know that an important Christian leader like Luther faced deep spiritual struggles?

    Many good books and articles have been written about Luther. You might do some extra reading on his life ahead of time. This question gives participants the chance to relate to a famous Christian leader. This question can help participants feel more normal—all people face spiritual struggles.

2. Why do we have trouble showing ourselves grace? How can we make the shift from guilt to grace?

    Discuss what it means to show grace to ourselves and others. As Christians, we can think beyond simply "Don't be so hard on yourself." Lift their sights to see that Christ extends grace to us, and we can move from guilt to grace by holding on to Christ's forgiveness.

3. Share your understanding of the word *righteousness*. How does the Christian concept of righteousness give comfort?

    Remind participants of the righteousness that gave Luther comfort, the alien righteousness outside of himself. Stay centered on the Gospel. The comfort of righteousness is the comfort of being a Christian, saved by grace through faith in Christ.

4. When people call Christians self-righteous or judgmental, what words or behaviors do they point to as evidence? What might Christians do to prove these labels inaccurate?

   Ask if any participants have been called self-righteous or judgmental or if they have seen these accusations leveled at other Christians. Invite group members to share their stories, not as complaints but to relate the question to personal experience. For the second question, guide participants to think of ways they can serve or show humility.

5. The Barna study compared pharisaical attitudes and actions to Christlike attitudes and actions. Give an example of Christlike words or behavior you've encountered over the past week.

   Review what, according to the survey, was considered Jesus-like behavior and Pharisee-like behavior. Concentrate on the positive, the Christlike behaviors. This question provides a great opportunity to shine a light on a group member or someone else as an example of faith lived out.

6. Which do you think is a bigger problem for Christians: guilt or self-righteousness? How about for you? Explain your answers.

   Review the concepts of guilt and self-righteousness. This question can provide insight into the spiritual struggles of group members. Discuss the role of self-deception in both types of struggles. Remind participants that Christ is their righteousness, removing their guilt and eliminating their need to justify themselves.

7. Pride lurks in every human heart. How do we guard our hearts against pride?

   Both guilt and self-righteousness can be tied to pride. Guilt is failing to live up to our own high expectations; self-righteousness is an inflated ego. Discuss ways to cultivate humility. Allow time for participants to share specific examples of how they've battled pride in their own hearts.

8. How might it change people if they saw their sins as pebbles and Christ's righteousness as an immovable rock that outweighs all sins?

   Discuss the freeing power of God's grace. What effect would that freedom have on how we think and act? Reinforce that Christ's righteousness *is* the immovable rock that outweighs all sins!

CHAPTER 3

1. If you made a list of the most stressful events in life, what would be on it?

    Depending on the size of the group, you might ask for an example from each participant. Express empathy for the stressful events people have experienced.

2. What stresses are you facing now?

    Here are some ways to identify stressful events: What causes you to lose sleep? What worries you? When do you feel under pressure? This question allows group members to understand what it's like to be in one another's shoes.

3. Tell about a time you braced yourself for something stressful. Did your preparations soften the impact?

    Participants might recall a time they prayed to prepare their hearts for an anxious situation. Or they might recall seeking counsel or rehearsing what to say in a difficult conversation. In some cases, preparation may have softened the impact. In other cases, such as the death of a loved one, it's impossible to fully prepare our hearts.

4. What do you find to be peaceful? It might be a favorite place, a relaxing activity, or something else.

    This question shifts the focus from the negative (stress) to the positive (peace). Encourage participants to identify what makes something peaceful. Quiet? No responsibility? Predictability?

5. Compare the three kinds of peace mentioned in the chapter: the peace offered by the world, the peace offered by the devil, and the peace offered by Christ.

   The world offers a fleeting peace based on circumstances. The devil offers false peace through avoidance and counterfeit solutions. Christ's peace transcends circumstances; it's real and lasting.

6. Would you rather be exempt from hard times or have a companion in those times? Explain your choice.

   At some point, everyone probably wishes for an exemption from suffering. Discuss the benefits of going through hard times with the Holy Spirit by your side.

7. Name some lies that steal peace. Name some truths that restore peace.

   The chapter mentions anger, regret, and anxiety as obstacles to peace. What causes those emotions for your group members? The list of Scriptures in the Storehouse of Spiritual Weaponry is a collection of truths that restore peace.

8. Have you ever doubted God's presence? Have you ever felt God's presence? In either or both cases, describe your experience.

   Those who have doubted God's presence may wish to explain what caused doubt and how they've worked through doubts. Those who have felt God's presence may wish to describe how a person "feels" God's presence. For a question inviting subjective answers, there is no right or wrong answer, although some responses may need to be examined more closely based on God's Word.

CHAPTER 4

1. Do you feel the world is becoming more dangerous? How so?

   Encourage specific examples. The question assumes that the world is becoming more dangerous, but some may feel the world is becoming safer. Accept all answers as valid opinions.

2. What makes you feel safe? unsafe?

   Participants may talk about physical safety. They also might share what makes them feel emotionally safe or unsafe. For example, words of affirmation can make us feel safe, while being around someone who has hurt us in the past can make us feel unsafe.

3. What are some spiritual doubts you've wrestled with?

   Some doubts may come across as purely intellectual. Others may clearly be born out of personal loss or pain. Be prepared for feelings underlying doubts, such as anger toward God for a tragic loss.

4. Describe a time when Satan leveraged a hardship to attack your faith.

   As the leader, you might assist participants in making connections between a personal hardship and the work of Satan. You might identify lies about God, others, or themselves that people have believed as a result of hardships. Examples might include feeling that a particular hardship is all your fault when it's really not or

believing that you're suffering because God is angry with you.

5. We do an injustice to people in their spiritual journey if we judge them for their doubts. How do we appropriately give people space for doubts and questions about God?

    You might invite participants to share faith questions or doubts they've had. What kind of space did they need to work through their questions or doubts? What helped them in that portion of their faith journey? What hindered them in wrestling with doubts or questions?

6. In several places, God is described as a shield. What does it mean to you that God is your shield?

    What does a shield do? How is that like God? The question invites personal application. God isn't just a shield; He's *your* shield.

7. Tell about a time when others stood shoulder to shoulder with you and helped you through a struggle.

    This is a great time for participants to acknowledge individuals who have supported them. Remind everyone that those people are gifts from God, sent by God in His perfect timing and wisdom. If appropriate, you might encourage participants to find an opportunity to thank that person, even if a long time has passed. In addition, you might consider ways group members can stand shoulder to shoulder and support one another in a current situation.

8. At the end of His conversation with Thomas in John 20, Jesus said, "Blessed are those who have not seen and yet have believed" (v. 29). What do those words mean to you? How do you see yourself in that promise?

   Affirm that faith is a form of seeing Jesus, just as saving and valid as seeing Him in the flesh as the disciples did. Explore what it means to be blessed and how it feels to know that God blesses you, or shows favor to you, because of His love for you in Jesus.

CHAPTER 5

1. What do you think is a favorite corner of people's minds where Satan tends to set up shop? Where are you most vulnerable to deception and misdirection?

   Think in terms of categories, such as relationships, work, the past, the future, or finances, to name a few. Be prepared; some might share very specifically about personal experiences with deception and misdirection.

2. On a scale of 1 to 10 (with 1 being "not hopeful at all" and 10 being "extremely hopeful"), how hopeful are you? Do you tend to be more optimistic or pessimistic?

   Follow up by asking participants why they picked the number they did. Ask for examples of times they've been optimistic or pessimistic.

3. Colossians 3:15 tells us, "Let the peace of Christ rule in your hearts." How might the peace of Christ rule more fully in your life? Think about specific areas in your life, such as home, friendships, the workplace, finances, and health.

   This is a good time for people to share what's troubling them in different areas of life. Encourage participants to think of how they can turn over their worries to the Lord, trading anxiety for His peace.

4. Are you waiting for God's deliverance? What is hard about waiting for "that day"?

   Ask participants to identify a current reason for waiting. It could be waiting for medical test results, for a job, for a wayward child to return to the faith, or for any

number of things. Discuss why it's a challenge to not have what you desire but still hope for it.

5. How can your waiting become more faith filled and productive?

    This question invites participants to consider how to grow in faith and love during seasons of waiting. Encourage them to choose a topic to study for personal growth or to embrace an act of service toward others, among other possibilities.

6. What topics do you feel get the most attention in sermons? What would you like to hear more about? Consider sharing your list with your pastor.

    As group leader, you can compile everyone's answers to share with your pastor. You can gather more information by asking why they chose certain topics.

7. Have you ever memorized Scripture? Tell about a time when a Bible verse came to mind.

    You might ask the group for any tips on memorizing Scripture: how to choose a verse, how to commit it to memory, and the like. This question could lead to some powerful sharing, as participants demonstrate the power of God's Word for real life.

8. Choose one of the sample memory verses from this chapter and explain how it's helpful for you as you live for Christ.

    You might suggest choosing one of these verses as a starting place for Scripture memorization. As a group challenge, everyone could recite their selected verses next time.

CHAPTER 6

1. Hebrews 4:15 states, "For we do not have a high priest who is unable to sympathize with our weaknesses, but one who in every respect has been tempted as we are, yet without sin." What comfort do you find in knowing that Jesus faced temptation just as we do?

    This question is a chance to establish common ground between our experiences as human beings and Jesus' experience as fully human (while still fully God). Is it surprising to know that Jesus Himself faced temptation?

2. Have you ever struggled with being too passive? Share as you're comfortable doing so.

    It may be helpful to define *passive*. Sometimes patience or quiet observation are mistaken for passivity. The group might explore what causes people to be passive—that is, failing to be assertive when a situation calls for action.

3. Do you normally consider yourself a fighter? What makes that term feel natural or unnatural based on your personality?

    This question provides a good opportunity for group members to hear one another's self-perceptions. Often, people have a different perception of themselves than others have of them.

4. Identify an area in your life in which you need to exhibit more of a fighting spirit.

You might ask for examples of when a fighting spirit might have changed the outcome of a situation. Taking the question further, you could prompt participants to envision what their lives might look like going forward with more of a fighting spirit.

5. How can you tell whether a Bible verse is being used correctly or is being taken out of context? Can you think of a time when you had to make that distinction?

All kinds of words can be taken out of context, such as a sound bite on the evening news, extracted from a speech, and presented in a way that the speaker didn't intend. In the same manner, people can present Bible verses as saying something that doesn't fit the theme and intent of a passage. For example, someone might share a verse about good works and suggest that we're saved by works, which contradicts the Gospel.

6. "No temptation has overtaken you that is not common to man. God is faithful, and He will not let you be tempted beyond your ability, but with the temptation He will also provide the way of escape, that you may be able to endure it" (1 Corinthians 10:13). What do you understand this verse to mean?

It's possible to think that we can resist temptation through our own willpower. Instead, keep the focus on God's faithfulness and provision during times of temptation. A true understanding of this verse comforts us and helps us to rely more fully on the Lord to strengthen us against temptation.

7. Jesus encountered temptation armed with the truth that He is God's Son. How can your status as God's child help you withstand temptation?

   Consider what it means to be a child of God. Discuss the benefits of being God's child, including the security that faith gives us.

8. We've studied the six pieces that constitute the armor of God. Which piece of the armor do you need most right now? Explain why.

   Review the six pieces of armor. Name the pieces and go into some detail about what each piece signifies. Then invite participants to explain which piece they feel is most needed for them right now.

CHAPTER 7

1. On a scale of 1 to 10 (with 1 being "weak" and 10 being "strong"), how would you rate your prayer life?

    Not everyone will have the same personal definition of a strong prayer life. The frequency of prayer that one person ranks as a 3 might rank as a 7 for someone else. Allow for complete subjectivity in answers.

2. When do you normally pray during the day? Describe any routines or disciplines you have related to prayer.

    This is a good time for participants to get ideas from one another about prayer routines and disciplines. It's important that those without a strong prayer life aren't deflated with shame, and that those with strong prayers lives aren't inflated with pride. Emphasize that God loves all of us, regardless of how we spend our time. Along with that, it is God's desire that we grow in faith and commune with Him regularly in prayer.

3. What do you think are the most common excuses not to pray?

    Some possible answers are "I don't know what to say," "I'm too busy," and "God never answers my prayers."

4. In the Garden of Gethsemane, the disciples failed to pray because they were exhausted from sorrow. What exhausts you? What replenishes you?

    Pay careful attention to these answers. Participants may give helpful tips about how to meet their emotional needs. Everyone is wired differently.

5. In the Garden of Gethsemane, angels attended Jesus to strengthen Him. Tell about a time when God strengthened you amid adversity.

   Explore what it looks like for God to strengthen a believer. Here are some examples: He gives physical energy. He sustains a person's resolve to press on. He gives a new and better perspective on a person's circumstances. Encourage participants to give their testimonies of God's strength in their lives.

6. What expectations do we place on God when we pray to Him? Which of our expectations are fair, and which are unfair?

   One expectation might be that God is obligated to grant our wishes if He truly loves us. Another expectation might be that God will consider our prayers but ultimately do what He determines is best. Allow participants to decide what they feel are fair and unfair expectations.

7. The Bible instructs us to "rejoice always, pray without ceasing, give thanks in all circumstances; for this is the will of God in Christ Jesus for you" (1 Thessalonians 5:16–18). What do you understand these words to mean, particularly the command to pray without ceasing?

   Direct participants away from being too focused on the time element. ("How can you pray without ceasing? You can't stop life and pray 24-7!") Focus them instead on the mindset and heart orientation behind praying without ceasing—the faith behind it, faith that is created and sustained by the Holy Spirit dwelling in us.

8. Dedicate a few minutes to fight for others in prayer!

   If participants are comfortable praying aloud, you might ask each person to pray for the person seated on his or her left (or right). You also could ask for prayer requests and lead the prayer yourself. The point is that everyone is prayed for individually.

CONCLUSION

1. If someone said to you, "I'm having a hard time forgiving myself," what would you say to comfort that person? How could you apply the content of the chapter to someone who struggles to fully embrace Jesus' gift of forgiveness?

    This question is worded in such a way that participants can share personal struggles without necessarily revealing that they are the ones struggling. Listen carefully for obstacles to accepting forgiveness for themselves. At every opportunity, affirm that Jesus' sacrifice on the cross is total, covering all sins.

2. Our feelings don't always match up with our beliefs. Why do you think our feelings are so capable of leading us astray from the truth?

    It would be helpful to think of an example of when this is true. When do people get carried away by their feelings? When do feeling and truth not match up? Explore why feelings have such a strong power of distortion. Remind participants that we base our trust on the truth of God's Word, even when emotions fail us.

3. The chapter states, "Perhaps the most difficult spiritual battle we fight is to fully embrace Jesus' gift of forgiveness *for us*." Do you agree or disagree? Explain your answer.

    Participants may feel that another spiritual battle is more difficult; make certain that they feel welcome to express their viewpoint. Explore what makes some spiritual battles extremely difficult.

4. This chapter highlighted several people in the Bible who may have struggled to forgive themselves. Which of them do you think had the hardest time releasing guilt?

    For more background on these people, you may wish to assign readings in advance of, during, or after the study.

    > Paul—Acts 9:1–19
    >
    > Peter—Luke 22:31–34, 54–62
    >
    > Samson—Judges 16:1–22
    >
    > Moses—Numbers 20:1–13
    >
    > David—2 Samuel 11:1–27

5. The Bible speaks of "forgetting what lies behind and straining forward to what lies ahead" (Philippians 3:13). How do these words apply to you? What are you straining forward to right now?

    Some participants will be more comfortable than others at naming what they're leaving behind. Answers could be very personal. What they're straining toward is likely to be a hopeful answer. Affirm and encourage them as they pursue their goals with the help of the Holy Spirit. Check in at a later date to see how the "straining forward" is going.

6. Grandmotherly wisdom says, "If you're having a bad day, do something for someone else and you'll feel better." Have you experienced this to be true? Give an example.

    Affirm participants for their acts of service, no matter how big or small. Ask how serving others made them feel, particularly if they were having a bad day.

7. Generate ideas about specific ways you can love "in deed and in truth" this week.

   You may want to compile a list and email the list to participants. Consider what it means to love in deed and truth.

8. Write three main takeaways you've gained from this book.

   Take a few minutes for everyone to write their answers. Then have participants share with one another.

ACKNOWLEDGMENTS

Thank you to Concordia Publishing House for the opportunity to publish this book and share its message. The entire team at CPH has been a joy to work with; special thanks to Laura Lane and Jamie Moldenhauer for your guidance and support. Thank you to those who graciously gave their time to review the manuscript and provide editorial feedback prior to submission: Alice Klement, Gary Larsen, Daniel Mueller, Melody Smith, and my mom, Dorothy Kennedy, a remarkable spiritual warrior. Thank you to my wife, Ashley, for your unwavering support through the spiritual battles; I'm blessed with an amazing partner in ministry and in life. To our children—Caleb, Ethan, Emma, and Zachary—your love gives me great strength each day. To my mom; my dad, Mike Kennedy; and my sister, Kelly Kennedy, thank you for your prayers and encouragement every step of the way. Thank you to the wonderful people of Shepherd of the Hills Lutheran Church, School, and Child Care for your faithfulness and steadfastness in all that we've experienced together as pastor and congregation. The Lord continues to guide us forward!